WOUNDED HOMECOMING

John Gallina & Dale Beatty

ISBN: 978-1-944027-48-3 (ebook)
ISBN: 978-1-944027-49-0 (paperback)

Published by Networlding Publishing
networlding.com

CONTENTS

Preface

John Gallina

Watercolor of Dale and John drawn by anonymous friend of Purple Heart Homes. "Greater love has no one than this, that he lay down his life for his friend." John 15:12

Acknowledgments

We are forever grateful to our dedicated Board of Directors. To my wife, Cori-Anne, and to Dale's wife, Belinda – who stood by us as we struggled to realize our mission of not leaving a soldier behind at home. Thank you to the entire Purple Heart Homes team – many of whom have worked with us since the early days of our organization. We are grateful to everyone who stepped up to help Purple Heart Homes get started. They worked without pay and brought professional skills to our organization that we could not possibly afford. To all of the volunteers who gave their time and energy to improving the lives of our service-connected disabled veterans – you are all a critical component of our mission. To Melanie Balousek – who was asked to assist with editing this book just days after she was hired to Purple Heart Homes – thank you for your diligence to this project. We are extraordinarily grateful to Melissa Wilson and her team at Networlding Publishing Inc. for working with us to turn the idea of this book into a reality. Last but certainly not least – thank you to BooneOakley for your creative and capable staff who are so good at helping Purple Heart Homes with our style. We are blessed.

Finding Your Passion and Purpose from Reading our Book

As Dale and I traveled and spoke to audiences about our journey together as combat wounded Iraq veterans, we had so many people come up to us and ask how they could get involved with Purple Heart Homes or how they could start their own nonprofit. We became more aware of how important it is to have purpose and meaning in our lives and in our jobs.

In fact, we realized how starting Purple Heart Homes to help veterans live safely and with dignity in their own homes helped both of us heal and reintegrate as we overcame physical and emotional injuries.

Dale was injured severely and spent a year at Walter Reed Army Medical Center learning how to walk on prosthetic legs. He never complained to me about being a double amputee. He always had an amazing, positive, can-do attitude. Dale wanted privacy at home. Behind closed doors, he took off his prosthetics in order to let his legs rest and heal after walking on them all day.

Dale gathered his passion from older veterans who admired his spirit, ability to articulate clearly how we were injured, and the importance of sharing our mission. While at Walter Reed, a Korean War double amputee would visit him and Dale told me, "He gave me hope. If he could adapt, then I could adapt, too." He recognized that no matter when or where you served, all veterans are alike. Many veterans struggle with needing help from the community to build a ramp, paint a house, or widen doorways to put in a walk-in shower.

While helping other veterans, his own spirit was lifted when he saw others inspired by his attitude and work.

Dale, just before first movement from Kuwait crossing into Iraq

For me, I suffered from the invisible injuries of war. I experienced not only back and head injuries but suffered from a traumatic brain injury and post-traumatic stress. I had a real problem with my short-term memory. I often thought that I had a sentence structure in place, and then it would just leave my mind. It was gone, and I became frustrated when my memory failed me.

Making the decision to start our nonprofit – Purple Heart Homes – helped me focus. It forced me to think. When I returned home, a social worker from the VA helped me learn the importance of writing things down immediately so I would not forget. I learned how to take notes for everything – using sticky notes to help me remember things from picking up my daughter from a play date to attending an appointment or an important meeting. Reading became a rehab practice as well to develop better word recall and structure.

I would be less than honest if I said that starting a nonprofit is easy. It is difficult, but if you have drive, a clearly stated mission, and values combined with purpose, it can be done. Dale and I have always said that if two Artillerymen from North Carolina with a high school education can start a nonprofit, and you have a cause that you are passionate about – you can do it, too. In order to find your purpose – you first must experience it first, just as we did.

John, outside of the barracks in Iraq at FOB Summerall

Stories About Veterans Lives We Committed to Help

In this first book of the *Wounded Homecoming* series, we have included some stories about the approved veterans we helped to renovate their homes and to enable them to become first time responsible homeowners.

As you read their stories, you will see how their commitment to serve our country impacted and changed their lives forever.

When Dale and I were deployed, we thought about just wanting to 'be home.' To a veteran, home means everything. When you serve in the military, your home changes from base to base and from deployment to deployment. The change of address impacts veteran families as kids must adapt to new schools and new surroundings. There is not the same stability one gets from living in the same home with the same zip code for many years.

To a veteran, a home is a sanctuary – a place to feel safe and secure. A home to a veteran provides much needed healing and stability. Every community plays an important role in welcoming home our military; America is home.

As you read each veteran's story, you will learn how their experience changed them and shaped their lives. You will learn how having a home adapted to meet their needs and interacting with the volunteers in the community helped the healing process. As many of our veterans healed their visible and invisible injuries, we found they, too, wanted to pay it forward – to give back to others and to have that important sense of purpose in their life.

Learning More About Our Story

Dale and I cover the story of our 22-year friendship in the early chapters of the book. We share stories of our journey from the time we enlisted in the North Carolina National Guard at age 17, to our deployment to Iraq, to starting Purple Heart Homes. What we did not mention is how important timing and strategic positioning worked to our advantage.

When we returned home injured in 2005, the war in Iraq and Afghanistan was front page news. We were thanked for our service by grateful Americans. Even though only one percent of the population volunteered to serve in Iraq and Afghanistan, the media covered events unfolding with the wars on a daily basis.

We were amazed by the number of post 9/11 nonprofit organizations that were created to help only returning Iraq and Afghanistan veterans. We recognized that it was the older veterans that served in the wars fought before us that helped ensure that we would have benefits they did not have and that we would be thanked and recognized for our service and sacrifice.

When we decided to start Purple Heart Homes, we wanted to raise awareness about the many housing challenges faced by veterans and their caregivers. Many veterans live in homes that often are not suited for service-connected disabilities combined with normal aging issues experienced later in life. As a result of those disabilities and fixed incomes, they can no longer make needed repairs themselves.

Nearly 50 percent of all veterans are age 65 and older. The Department of Veterans Affairs projects senior veterans age 65 and older will makeup at least 40 percent of all veterans for the next 25 years, a population of over nine million veterans.

Purple Heart Homes became one of the few nonprofits started by two combat wounded Iraq veterans focused on helping veterans of all generations. It became a very strong positioning advantage that helped us generate a great deal of national media attention.

We were featured in the August 29, 2011, issue of TIME magazine in a cover story written by Joe Klein called, "Meet the New Greatest Generation." Klein said, "A new kind of war meant a new set of skills. Now veterans from Iraq and Afghanistan are bringing leadership lessons home, where we need them most." There were five of us featured in that cover story. Dale and I were described by Klein as "having true grit" for starting Purple Heart Homes in 2008 "for the betterment of their communities."

That cover story in TIME magazine lead to other national news stories about Dale and I starting Purple Heart Homes, including articles in Reader's Digest, AARP, CNN, FOX, and a special ABC Nightline segment that ran during prime time on the ABC television network featuring Bob Woodruff, who followed us on location to some Vietnam veterans' homes and to a paralyzed Afghanistan veteran's home that we worked on.

As you can well imagine, that helped put us on the national map.

Know that when you buy our book – 100% of the proceeds are going towards Purple Heart Homes to enable us to continue our mission of providing more housing solutions that improve veterans' lives one home at a time.

In Memoriam – Dale Beatty

As Dale and I traveled the country together sharing our story, seeking funding and sponsorships for Purple Heart Homes, everyone told us that we should write a book.

It took us two years and a lot of time and help from others to put our collective thoughts together in an organized manner.

We finally submitted our manuscript to our publisher, when just days later on Monday, February 12, 2018, my battle buddy, Dale Beatty, died unexpectedly from a double pulmonary embolism.

Dale was born in Statesville, North Carolina, on August 7, 1978. He leaves behind his wife, Belinda, and his sons, Dustin and Lucas, and a little daughter, Sophia.

Dale was awarded the Purple Heart Medal from President George W. Bush during his time at Walter Reed. He also received the Army Commendation Medal and the Army Achievement Medal (3OLC). Dale was named a Top Ten CNN Hero in 2013. He received the Congressional Medal of Honor Foundation Citizens Award in 2014, the Carolina's Freedom Foundation Patriotism Award in 2011, and the Hope for the Warriors Hope and Courage award.

Dale sat on the board of directors for Fisher House Foundation. He was also the drummer in his band, Outlaw 21.

There is not a day that goes by that I do not think of Dale and our meaningful journey in life we shared together. A big part of me also died when Dale passed so suddenly. We made it back from Iraq. We were ready to celebrate our tenth year as a successful nonprofit.

I miss his grin, quick wit, positive attitude, and how he signed off on all email and text messages to me with "roger that."

What is a battle buddy? In the military, you are assigned a battle buddy, or a partner that is expected to assist you mutually as your partner in and out of combat. The relationship developed between battle buddies is unlike any relationship you can ever have. It is different than a mother and her child. It is different than simply being best friends. The relationship is so intertwined because your life is in the hands of your battle buddy on and off the battlefield.

This book is dedicated to my battle buddy – Dale Beatty.

Dale, standing on a ladder inside Purple Heart Homes' warehouse

Introduction

John Gallina

While this book contains both collective and individual stories, Dale and I will share with you our current mission and hope that, by the time you finish, you can truly recognize the individual and societal impact of a few ideas that have led us to an innovative vision and philosophy that completes and gives our lives purpose. We hope you enjoy the stories we've assembled for you to better understand the lives of veteran families everywhere. These stories are our inspiration to continue our mission.

Dale and I wrote this book through the eyes of two combat-wounded soldiers who have experienced firsthand the reintegration process and remain on a mission. However, we're far more than that. We are sons, brothers, husbands, and fathers, who recognize a wrong that needs righting. We hope to leave behind something that can make a lasting impact on this country we love so much. After our time in Iraq, and as civilians now, we're still battle buddies. We were trained not to leave a comrade on the field of battle, yet there are so many veterans who are left alone to struggle at home. Undervalued, damaged, perhaps unwanted, and left without hope—these veterans need a battle buddy of their own.

What is a battle buddy? It's an Army term used as implied: it's the buddy system, and in the world of a fighter pilot, it's a wingman. Still, what does it *really* mean? In combat, it's knowledge that you've got someone by your side who will face down the dangers of the battlefield. When fear and doubt creep in and replace thoughts of action and reason, your battle buddy says, "We can do this," with just a glance.

Coffee with Heroes

Richard Warren was a helicopter gunship pilot in Vietnam. He came home to North Carolina after the war. The way he was treated—often ignored or reproached by the community in his own hometown—hurt him so badly that he moved to Germany, where he lived for most of his adult life. It was only when his mother became ill that Richard returned home to take care of her. After he settled in, he opened a coffee shop called Pat's, named after his wife, in downtown Mooresville. Passionate about helping veterans like himself, Richard started offering free coffee to all veterans on Thursdays. It was his goal to welcome every new veteran, as well as current veterans, into his shop in the way he never was after Vietnam. As a result of his giveback to the community, it wasn't long before veterans started to congregate there. Their numbers grew each week. Besides sharing war stories, the veterans were building their own vibrant community, bringing in their memorabilia to share with Richard and his growing customer base. They turned the coffee shop into a sort of living museum. A ton of healing occurred there because of his efforts.

Unfortunately, Richard passed away in May 2009 due to heart problems associated with exposure to Agent Orange in Vietnam. He had been in the process of forming a charity called Welcome Home Veterans before he died, and his loyal group of veteran customers stepped up to the plate to help. After meeting at the old Bob Evans restaurant for a month, several veterans got together and leased some space on South Main Street, naming it Richard's Coffee Shop in Richard's honor. From there, the growth of the coffee shop continued. Volunteers pitched in to run the daily operations and fundraising efforts.

Dale and I would go on Thursdays when we could. It was around our third visit when we met Len, a kind, quick-witted veteran of World War II, and immediately took a liking to him. Len unknowingly had become one of the patriarchs of the place. He was part of a group of older World War II veterans who mostly didn't leave their homes except to drive to church on Sunday and the coffee shop on Thursday.

*Dale receives an education from a distinguished
veteran at Richard's Coffee Shop*

It was on their cherished Thursdays when the veterans would take
their walkers, hobble to their cars, and make the short but very important trip to the coffee shop to hang out with their fellow veteran

buddies. Dale and I think they realized that one Thursday visit could easily be their last. So, we watched these guys who weren't always in the best physical shape or strength, make a concerted effort to get into a safe haven and place of comrades.

There were a couple of steps going into the back door that were awkward for everyone who used them. Most people used that entrance, and for some the steps created a hazard, with a number of the people falling down and hurting themselves as they tried to enter. One Thursday, Dale and I saw one guy struggling with his walker as he attempted to navigate the stairs. He fell over suddenly, smashing his face on the floor. We were horrified and rushed to his aid. Later on, we said to one another, "Damn, it's not that hard to build a ramp."

Like clockwork, the shouting began with "at ease" for the 10:00 a.m. weekly announcements, as those in charge tried to quiet down the fifty conversations that were taking place. The first order of business brought up was the fact that yet another World War II veteran had fallen, and as the question was asked, "Well, what are we going to do about it?" I made eye contact with Dale, who already knew what the next words out of my mouth would be: We'll build the ramp. As Dale stepped up beside me, I gestured to us and challenged the leadership committee, "Here's your free labor if you buy the materials." A few laughs went around the room, and the big Marine in charge looked down at us and replied with his own challenge: "Ha! We've been talking about that for months. When can you start?"

Dale and I replied without hesitation, "Tomorrow."

Over the next few days, we got a group of volunteers together, bought all the necessary supplies, and poured a concrete accessible ramp. The following Thursday, as we were working on the handrails, Len approached the back door early as usual. Walking up and down the ramp a few times, he seemed pleased and said, "Boys, you really did a good job getting that ramp built. I really appreciate that. It makes it easier for me to walk in."

Since then, the coffee shop has grown exponentially: over 16,000 veterans from all over the world have visited. This community of veterans has continued to grow, to the point where they were forced to move down the street to a larger location, directly across from where the original Pat's coffee shop was located.

Richard's Coffee Shop

Truly now, Richard's vision is achieved in the warm welcome that greets every new face when they walk through those doors. Richard's picture hangs on the wall, overlooking the room where veterans continue to gather, even though they may not always know the origin of the story.

*John and Dale take a moment to reflect on the completed
ramp after veterans use it for the first time.*

Len's Story

Len was a major war hero, in our opinion and by others' estimation. He was always humble and gracious; he became an inspiration to us. He showed a true affection toward us younger veterans, saying often, "You guys are my heroes." To a young veteran, there was no greater honor than someone from the greatest generation looking at them as a peer.

Len's story is amazing. He was drafted into World War II, and while hitchhiking to the recruitment station, he got a ride from an Air Force captain. That captain happened to be Chuck Yeager, the very man who would become a World War II fighter ace in his own right and the first person to break the sound barrier in 1947.

Inspired by Yeager's journey, along with the others he came into contact with, Len soon became a lieutenant, leading men into battle. In fact, he was with Ernie Pyle, the famous war correspondent, when Pyle was killed during the battle of Okinawa.

During the war, Len's unit was often crowded onto troopships when attempting to make amphibious landings on the many fiercely defended islands they assaulted during the Pacific campaigns. During one such landing, the artillery from the naval guns would attack the defensive positions on the island, which, theoretically, kept the landing craft from being attacked. The shelling would continue until the last possible instant in order to establish a beachhead. Unfortunately, the island defenders were so well entrenched in caves that the shelling had little effect, and they rained down a desperate and treacherous retaliation of mortar shells, small arms, and coastal guns on the Allied forces attempting the landing.

Several attempts at landing led to mounting casualties and a still-unoccupied beach. Len and a sergeant volunteered to charge the beach with flamethrowers and torch the enemy as they came out of the caves so that the rest of their men could make a landing when the firing let up—basically a suicide mission. It was a blessing that somehow Len and the sergeant were successful.

When a guy like Len calls a younger veteran his hero, and the younger veteran shares the same reverence for him, it's profound. Here's a guy who's an exemplary man of World War II. How can he not have post-traumatic stress from an experience like that? If he didn't tell you about it, you wouldn't know. He looks like every other grandfatherly figure. Yet, when this person ends up sharing stories of remarkable heroism and courage in the face of war, it gives you the opportunity to begin to understand the depth of the experience that is going into war and then coming home. There is a two-hundred-year timeline of experiences by millions of men and women like Len who have served our country with honor and distinction. Many have returned home without a warm and grateful welcome. What Dale and I find to be a critical challenge is helping people like Len not only return home safely, but create a healing environment for him and other veterans like him.

John, smiling with veterans of World War II: Len McCutcheon to the right, Hub Knox in the center, and Harry Hart on the left.

Inspirations

Dale and I continue to heal from our injuries—physical, emotional, and psychological — alongside guys like Len. We've discovered that there is no question whether or not older veterans love Iraq and Afghanistan veterans. When a World War II veteran looks at us and tells us that we're his heroes, it brings tears to our eyes. It lets us know that we're on the right path.

Literally hundreds of stories of service, sacrifice, and sometimes pain and heartache accompany the veterans we meet on our mission. It is those veterans who Dale and I now serve and who are always at the forefront of our minds. They're the reason we decided to come together and tell the story of our journey in this book, as well as the stories of a number of veterans we've had the honor of serving at Purple Heart Homes, the nonprofit organization we started in 2008. We're proud to say that by the end of 2017, Purple Heart Homes had made improvements to over three hundred veteran homes across the nation and started chapters in ten states. And the organization continues to grow every month.

In this book, Dale and I will share stories with you of veterans from different generations, the conflicts they served in, their injuries, their recoveries, their return to their families and communities, and their varied experiences of life after war. We hope that after reading these stories you will come to recognize that all veterans can't be seen or understood in the same way. Each veteran's story is individual and personal—a product of their time, the particular circumstances of their service, and the realities of their return home.

Additionally, we want to shed light on the common challenges all veterans face: psychological, emotional, physical, financial, and more. We want you to understand the impact these issues have on the veterans' parents, spouses, children, and friends, and their larger communities. More importantly, we want to share with you the impact that our innovative programs provide, and suggest ways you can get involved to make our communities stronger.

Our hope is that this book will create a dialogue in communities around the United States, so that families and friends of veterans will better understand their challenges and find ways to support these great Americans. So, come along and meet a few of the amazing men and women we've come to know, and discover how two soldiers and legions of volunteers are creating a nationwide movement to provide all generations of veterans housing support—and more.

John [kneeling] beside World War II veteran,
Hub Knox, prior to a Memorial Day gathering.

CHAPTER 1

From BB Guns to Howitzers

Dale Beatty

John and I both grew up in the same rural county in North Carolina during the 1980s, watching TV shows like *G.I. Joe* and *The A-Team*. We're about the same age. Both of us checked out the Army/Navy store often, or spent time crashing through the woods and creeks with our BB guns. We were both enamored with our relatives who had served in the military. The schools and churches we attended, the values we were taught, and pretty much everything else in our daily routines were similar—but we didn't know each other yet.

Military service is part of our shared heritage. Our grandfathers, great uncles, fathers, and uncles all served in the military in World War II, Korea, or Vietnam. I even remember stories of family members serving in World War I, the Civil War, and as far back as the American Revolution. Growing up, I saw their old uniforms hanging in their closets and became fascinated with their stories, though they rarely shared those stories with anyone. Looking back, I just knew that the look in their eyes and their quiet, but demanding presence had been forged on the battlefield.

Dale's great grandfather [left] standing with his squad during World War II

Dale poses at Richard's Coffee Shop with a photo of his great grandfather, John Davidson Miller, a World War I veteran

John's grandfather just before deployment to Korea in 1956

John's great uncle Grey and great aunt Ellen served
for over 20 years during the Cold War Era.

For both of us, serving in the military was just what you did. We were brought up expected to stand on the line of defense for our freedoms and preserve our rights, as well as to serve and protect those in need. And that's exactly what we did.

Real War Games in the Woods

During our sophomore and junior years in high school, we both started getting serious about joining the military. In the autumn of 1995, two local National Guard recruiters, SSG Hooker and SSG Richburg, visited our respective high schools. They discussed with both of us the prospect of joining the National Guard. They invited us to join a small group of other interested students from various schools around the county for a trip to Fort Bragg, a North Caro-lina military base. It was there that John and I first met and began to develop the camaraderie that has kept us friends for over twenty years now.

*John, at Basic Training graduation with
one of his Drill Instructors in 1997*

Dale's Basic Training photo

At Fort Bragg, we stayed in barracks that were built for World War II troops, the very same building we would later stay in before deploying to Iraq. These were the same barracks that our grandfathers and great uncles deployed through. We got to go into the field and become part of the unit that we were being recruited into, just like we would do if we were truly enlisted. They held mock training sessions where we were told, "This is some of what you'll learn in basic training. This is some of what you'll be expected to do as a soldier once you finish basic training."

There were sessions when they would teach us about first aid, troop movement, or how to call in a Medevac[1] report if somebody was hurt. They even put M-16s in our hands—but, of course, they had blanks, not real bullets. We were getting a firsthand glimpse, a taste of the dirt. We were gaining an understanding of what it was like to wear a real military uniform and carry a rifle and rucksack[2] through the woods—to really be a soldier. We were around other guys who had been in the military for twenty or thirty years. We got to ride in military vehicles with enlisted soldiers, not just a group from our school. The training had really started as a teaser, an attempt to reel us into the military lifestyle, which we were already drawn to because of our military heritage.

We both enlisted in March 1996, when we were seventeen years old, through a split-option training plan. After finishing school for the year, we'd go to basic training, return to school and graduate, then complete our advanced training during the following summer.

After we enlisted but before we went to basic training, we met for drill once a month with the recruiter and an assistant. During this period, we were called Rep 63s. They encouraged us to help recruit other people from our schools. Eventually, we each had three or four guys from our schools join us. The assistant recruiter, Doc, was a Vietnam veteran. He had served as a medic in a Special Forces unit. He had a very gruff, protective exterior, but he wanted to teach us. He reminded us of the importance of the things we'd learn that would keep us alive.

---

1 Medevac: the evacuation of military or other casualties to the hospital in a helicopter or airplane.

2 Rucksack: a bag with shoulder straps that allow it to be carried on someone's back, typically made of a strong, waterproof material and widely used by hikers; a backpack.

Learning from Doc, from a different generation, was interesting, fast-paced, often highly stressful, and several times, even scary. His first question to us during an improvised first-aid class was screamed loud enough to startle some and make others look. "Do you know how to treat a sucking chest wound, soldier?! Well, DO YOU?!" We were getting firsthand advice from somebody who had been there, who wore the combat infantryman badge[3] and had done or seen God knows what during combat in Vietnam. Doc often behaved like the war was going to start tomorrow, and maybe for him it hadn't quite ended. Regardless, his message came through to us loud and clear: this was no mere game we were attempting to play, and the skills we were learning early in our soldiering experience could one day mean the difference between life or death.

Interestingly, John and I didn't really like each other at first. We had attended rival high schools, so there was a lot of competitiveness between us. One of our first bonding experiences was when we went with a mutual friend and three other new recruits to the Coca Cola 600 NASCAR race at the Charlotte Motor Speedway to represent the North Carolina National Guard. We rode in a deuce and a half,[4] in the bed on troop seats, all the way there and back. We rode it onto the track with about fifty other servicemen and women from other branches. We held a huge American flag on the infield while the national anthem was playing. It was Memorial Day, and Lee Greenwood himself was singing the national anthem. We shared the infield with paratroopers and helicopters from the 82nd Airborne Division and held the flag aloft reverently to the cheers of the crowd.

Just being a small part of that occasion made pride and appreciation—for our flag, our country, and the people we defended—swell

---

3 Combat Infantry Badge: United States Army military award. The badge is awarded to infantrymen and Special Forces soldiers in the rank of Colonel and below, who personally fought in active ground combat while assigned as members of either an infantry, ranger, or Special Forces unit, of brigade size or smaller, any time after December 1941.

4 Deuce and a half: two-and-a-half-ton military cargo truck first used in World War II.

in our chests, and the crowd screamed their support of the same ideals. Holding our own section of the flag that represented so much sacrifice on Memorial Day elevated our patriotism and commitment, and added to the sensation of grandeur that youth brings. It was a day that burned bright in our hearts, and we needed as much of that extra boost as we could get for the next step in our military journey.

The Basics of Basic

John and I went to two different military bases for basic training, so we didn't experience that together. You might think you know what to expect in basic training, but the reality is that only some of what you expect actually happens. What you do experience ends up being different from the descriptions you hear by others. It was the first time either of us had been away from home on our own for a long period of time. We were treated as adults. We learned that nobody is responsible for you but you.

Dale, receiving his Basic Training graduation certificate

The best advice anybody can give you for basic training is to keep your mouth shut and do what you're told. Try to blend in. Another good piece of advice is to never volunteer for anything. There were certainly many lessons that came out of our experiences that neither of us anticipated, nor did we expect for these lessons to have such a cultural influence on us. The positives were huge, but we didn't have the full realization of that happening at the time.

John, at his Advanced Individual Training graduation in 1997

Basic Training lasted nine weeks. You experience a lot of new things, such as muscle failure, sleep deprivation, overly stressed situations, and even exhaustion as a result of pushing yourself to your physical and mental limits. During that time, phrases such as "pay attention to detail" and "if you see something, say something," are drilled into your head. Teamwork is key. Nobody wants to see the drill sergeant come by and the guy next to you gets in trouble. That means that you and the forty-five other guys in your unit are in trouble as well. This

41

could be something as simple as one button on your uniform being unbuttoned. Suddenly, you're all doing pushups for half an hour because one guy's button was unbuttoned, or just because the drill sergeant was in a bad mood, or he thought you needed to do some physical training.

Yeah, the drill sergeants yell at you. Yeah, you're all going to get punished because one guy did something wrong. All they're trying to do is get your mind and body fit, build a sense of camaraderie, and teach you how to take care of other people. The experience definitely helps you grow up. It teaches you to think of your actions and how they'll affect others around you, how to be responsible for the people to your left and right.

All of this played a critical role in molding John and me to be who we are today. We learned to care for our community. We learned to be willing to go into combat and put ourselves in harm's way for one another. After all of our training, we returned to civilian life and went to work. However, now we were trained soldiers to be called upon as needed.

The Life of a Guardsman

After basic and advanced training, our life was interspersed with donning the uniform of a soldier one weekend each month. We packed all our Army gear, went down to the armory, and either stayed there or went into the field for the weekend. We learned to go with the flow and to hurry up to wait. When we went into the field, everyone would get on a bus, drive down to Fort Bragg, go to motor pool, and draw our equipment, Howitzers,[5] and other track vehicles. Everyone would perform PMCS[6] and then go into the field to train for a day or day and a half. Oftentimes, we'd be given a field problem, or a battlefield scenario, which required us to work with various elements and follow tightly monitored tasks and protocols. All of these were measured for

---

5 Howitzer: a type of artillery piece characterized by a relatively short barrel and the use of comparatively small propellant charges to propel projectiles in relatively high trajectories, with a steep angle of descent.

6 PMCS: Preventive Maintenance Checks and Services.

safety, time, and accuracy. Even though we only wore our uniforms three or four days a month, we were expected to meet the same proficiency requirements of our active-duty counterparts.

Going into the field and putting camouflage on your face makes you think about your great-grandfather who served in the trenches of France, your grandfather in the fields of Germany, your uncles fighting in the jungles of Vietnam, and your sons, daughters, and grandchildren who may defend our country in wars to come. We may have started out imagining it that way, and more than likely it was a great part of the attraction, but what we soon began to experience was different. Once settled into that routine, we really began to see and understand the structure of the National Guard.

As members of Charlie Battery, I realized while assembling with the rest of the units in our state that there was great diversity. Although during our time artillery units were all male, I did recognize the newest composition of our military contained every race, color, and creed, as well as many females who served in transportation, medical, and support and service units. It wasn't just a bunch of white guys who liked guns and camping, as most would think. There were sisters and mothers serving right alongside us. They were tough and dependable soldiers just like us. In 2017, we saw the first integration of women into combat roles, even in the artillery. We've had quite the evolution in our military since the heroes I imagined in my youth served, and as the battlefield and landscape changes, so too do the ramifications of a homecoming.

Even though the military is very serious work, where you're often faced with imminent danger, someone in the unit will always bring humor to the situation. That would help build camaraderie. Then, there was the time-honored (now outlawed) tradition of hazing, most often out of love or boredom. Yes, we suffered through that and dished some out as well during our time.

For instance, when using a radio, a new private will come on and the sergeant will say, "Hey, private, go get me a can of radio squelch from the motor pool." Radio squelch is just the static sound you often hear on a two-way radio. You can't put it in a can, but the private doesn't know that. The private will ask the next sergeant for a can of radio squelch. The motor pool sergeant will play along, handing some random container of liquid for the return trip and eventually the private realizes that he is the butt of the joke. The best part is when you've been around long enough that some young soldier walks up to you and your role in the joke changes from unwilling participant to collaborator. Before any self-incrimination, we'll skip the part about the hazing uses of red or yellow paint.

For two or three weeks in the summer, you would go to one base or another for annual training. It might be Fort Stewart, Georgia or Fort Riley, Kansas or even the Mojave Desert if you were lucky. Usually held in May or June, Annual Training (AT) was guaranteed to be hot, exhausting, and a true recreation of battlefield conditions occurring in peak vacation time. All of your vehicles and equipment would be shipped to that base. You would start a two-week training exercise where you practice being proficient in a specific job. For John and I, that specific job was artillery. It was quite surreal to leave civilization behind, jam on those combat boots and helmet, and really have a chance to gain knowledge and an opportunity to work with your unit over a longer period of time. Charlie Battery was good. We were proficient and usually met or exceeded the requirements of our training. That's what we both did for six years. It was during those six years that we met many good friends, lost some of those good friends, fought some battles of bravado like young men do, and saw the world change on September 11, 2001.

Learning How to Blow Things Up

There are many different types of jobs in the military. You could become a human resources specialist, an aircraft pilot, or a cook, for example. You could join the infantry, artillery, or cavalry, or become combat engineers. Infantry is frontline foot soldiers. Artillery is second line because you're shooting over the infantry's heads.

Our jobs were to shoot a Howitzer, which is basically a huge rifle with 155 mm diameter bullets that weigh about a hundred pounds each. The barrel is more than sixteen feet long. A Howitzer can hit targets that range from three hundred meters to approximately twenty miles away. Howitzers are an old, conventional type of weaponry. They were used widely throughout both world wars, Korea, and Vietnam, and for a limited time during the Gulf War. Artillery fell out of favor as the weapon of choice for generals because aircraft, ships, and other long-range strike options incurred less risk on the battlefield, using fewer troops with faster, more targeted results. War had changed. Our job was really the old traditional World War II method of shooting artillery, but even that soon transitioned into the digital age, as we were the first National Guard unit to field the M109A6 Paladin.[7] The North Carolina guard had the distinction of being the first to field the brand-spanking new Paladins in 2000. We got to see the transition of war as conventional weapons were adapted to the digital age.

John snaps a photo of Dale manning a M2 .50 calibre machine gun at the National Training Center Ft. Irwin, CA.

---

7 M109A6 "Paladin": an American 155mm turreted self-propelled Howitzer, needing only a crew of four: the commander, driver, gunner, and an ammunition loader.

In training, we had Howitzer competitions, which were a rush. You're in competition with five other guns, each with a crew of five to eight people. You're given a fire mission and everyone is trying to shoot those hundred-pound bullets as fast as they can. It's a lot of hard work, but it's exhilarating to experience the sound, flash, and smoke, and the smell of the gunpowder.

John manning a M2 .50 calibre machine gun during training at Ft. Bragg, NC

There are a lot of job hazards involved with the Howitzer. If you're out in front of the gun when it goes off, you're definitely going to lose hearing, get knocked to the ground, and potentially be injured far worse than that. When you pull the trigger, the recoil is up to four feet at times, so someone standing in the wrong spot can easily be maimed or killed. During the process of loading it, when you close the seventy-pound spring loaded door—the breach—if your finger is in there, it's going to get cut off. On top of all the firing hazards, every so often you have to move the Howitzer and reset up to fire again, all timed and rated for precision.

The job was dangerous, to say the least. Our job was based on the

Cold War era thinking of the United States versus the Soviet Union. It assumed there would be a massive attack of troops, planes, tanks, and all the supporting equipment that goes along with that. Think of World War I, World War II, and Korea—trenches, observation posts, and a clear line of battle. In hindsight, it's interesting that our deployment to Iraq was nothing like what we spent years training for; we simply reverted back to the basics of soldiering. However, while there was no line or front, the combat zone was all around us. We were just small circles of bases surrounded by open hostile land, with only each other to depend on.

Disasters Strike

While the two of us served as guardsmen, there were multiple natural disasters that we responded to: two hurricanes (Fran in 1999 and Floyd in 2001), an ice storm, and a mountain flood due to rapid snow melt. During these types of events, when the governor declares a state of emergency, he calls up the National Guard on orders. Most of these activations are filled first by volunteers, and if there aren't enough volunteers, then a mandatory activation of entire units takes place. People have to leave their civilian jobs and assume their identity as a soldier in response to these disasters.

John and I both volunteered for duty during Hurricane Floyd. We loved getting out and being able to help; the activation duty seemed like it would be somewhat adventurous. All of those missions proved to be *very* adventurous. At that point, we hadn't trained in swiftwater rescue or flood evacuation, though we knew some basics and had done some rope courses—we could tie knots and drive a boat. It's a good thing we didn't mind wading in water up to our necks. This all gave new meaning to *Semper Gumby*.[8]

As a soldier, you're not necessarily trained for humanitarian missions, such as swiftwater rescue, or how to prevent suicide by cop.

---

8 *Semper Gumby*: a play on the official motto of the U.S. Marines and U.S. Coast Guard; refers to the animated clay character Gumby, meaning "*Always Flexible*"

Despite that fact, we faced all of these issues to help citizens in need, when called upon by the governor. We were trained to serve in a combat arms unit, and instead ended up helping entire communities with evacuations, rescues, transporting nurses and doctors over impossible bridges, and being the first to go into inaccessible areas. We answered the call with thousands of others to help our own with our fellow comrades from Old Hickory, the 30th Brigade of the North Carolina National Guard unit, to which our battalion belonged. The culture and training of the National Guard taught us to take care of and help other people. John and I prepared to go to war, but we were there to help people. To be comfortable with feeling uncomfortable begins in basic training, but witnessing the devastation to communities a mere three hours from our own homes showed us how fragile life really is in times of disaster.

When we arrived at a National Guard armory just outside Goldsboro, the water was only a few inches deep in some low-lying areas. The weather reports were predicting that the waters would go down and the hurricane would take a different route, but the governor felt that we should have Guardsmen standing ready. Within a few hours, we could tell that the water was rising. A lieutenant came through and said to us, "We got some pigs outside the armory that we want you to round up." Our friend, Willy, sprung up and took off. He ran around chasing these pigs, slipping, falling, and sliding through the mud while quite a few of us rolled around laughing. The next call pertained to some coffins that we needed to go catch—not such a laughing matter, as you can imagine. The preacher took us over to the church. It wasn't long before people were coming to the church just to ask for help.

Within about ten hours of us getting to Goldsboro, key leadership decided that we needed to evacuate the armory; we all needed to spread out to different places. They needed two or three volunteers to go to the fire department. John and I jumped up and said, "We'll take that one. We'll go out." They paired us up with a staff sergeant named Short. SSG Short was a man who didn't mince words. He told it like it was, and maintained his composure through the entire two-

and-a-half weeks. He drove us through nearly four feet of water in the Humvee to arrive at our new home: Marmac Volunteer Fire Department. This fire department took us in like we were family. They fed us, gave us beds, and took care of us. With every call for help that came into the fire department, the chief would come over to us and say, "We need you boys to go get them."

John and I took this five-ton truck and plowed through the water to retrieve people from their front porches, roofs, or hoods of their cars where they had been trapped by rising waters. Eventually, they got a boat for us, and with the volunteer firemen, we were zipping around the side streets of Goldsboro to ensure a safe ride to the Red Cross shelter for the people we rescued.

There was one mission that took place late at night, and water was rising quickly due to the heavy rain. One little community found itself now on a newly formed island. The road that led into the community resembled more of a boat slip. It ended where a lake had formed two days before. We were told, "You've got to go door-to-door and do a mandatory evacuation." It was predicted that the water was going to rise another eight feet that night. There was already six inches of water in the floors of these homes. John and I started going door-to-door and would say, "We're here to offer you a ride to the shelter and higher ground!"

We got down to the end of the street, knocked on a door, and nobody answered. However, we knew somebody was in there because we had been told that there was a guy in a wheelchair living there. We continued to knock and yell, "Hey, sir! We're North Carolina National Guard. We're here evacuating if you want a ride! We've got boats here and we can help you get your stuff together!"

This guy snatches the door open, pulls a pistol out from his lap, and points it at us. He said, "You bastards can't make me leave my house." It was as though he thought we were Stormtroopers throwing everybody out into the streets. Obviously, that was far from the case; we didn't even have weapons. We just said, "Sir, we're just asking. We're not telling you that you have to leave. We're asking and offering a ride." He replied, "I don't want no damn ride. I'm staying here." We left. We don't know what happened to that guy, but it was interesting to know the perception he had about us and what we were doing.

Later, the assistant fire chief told me that a neighbor called and said, "This woman is at the shelter. She has a son who is mentally disabled. He's not with her. We think he's still in the house." This man was left behind by his own mother to die in a house that we knew would soon be underwater.

John and I drove out on the boat, and found that the door was locked. We were yelling for this guy through windows that were all shut. The chief forced a fireman's axe into my hands and said, "Pop that door open." I complied and attempted to return the axe to the boat. The chief said, "Keep it, we don't know what state of mind this man is in." John and I shouldered the door open, in water up to our chests, calling out the name of the man assumed to be inside. It was eerie; carpet floats, and so does furniture sometimes. Afraid of everything we were bumping into or stepping on under the water, we waded through the house and continued calling out. When we arrived at the back bedroom, we heard a faint response. He finally answered us! He was on his mattress, under the covers, with only his head above the water. The mattress actually floated, which is the reason he was still alive. He was almost hypothermic. We retrieved him and took him back to the shelter.

I was so angry at the thought of this woman abandoning her own child. He was in his forties, but mentally he was probably eight years old.

While John and I had some tough missions, not all the days were that bad. The town had no power; it was running on generators. The guy who ran the grocery store came up to the fire station and said, "Look, you guys have power and you've got freezers here. Come and get all of the meat you want so we can feed people." The fire station started cooking and people came by to get a meal. The truth is that people in general will come together in times of need or shared suffering.

Our time in the National Guard really showed us the best and worst of what people go through and how we band together in times of crisis. The takeaway from this entire experience was that we saw our own state and fellow Americans devastated. These people lost everything. We were only nineteen years old and had whole families ask us, "Where can we go that's safe? What can we do?" A dad asked us, "What can I do to protect my family?" Our only answer was, "Get in this truck and we'll take you to shelter." It was life or death in some of these instances. We couldn't imagine what it would be like if our own homes were flooded. Seeing that loss of hope in people's eyes because they knew that they had lost everything due to the disruption of a natural disaster was heartbreaking.

Preparing for Iraq

Just before the 9/11 terrorist attacks happened, our National Guard unit was recognized as a readiness enhanced brigade. This meant that if a call came from the commander in chief, our unit would be one of the first Guard forces to deploy. Suddenly, John and I were doing additional training, receiving new equipment, and learning new skills. Then came 9/11, and it seemed inevitable that our unit would be deploying.

John and Cori-Anne pose for a photo just
after deployment ceremony in 2003.

The Minutemen were the original soldiers who most closely resemble our common National Guardsman and exist as our nation's oldest line of defense. Named for the expectation to assemble as a militia on the town square in one minute, they've been around since 1636, well before our Army was formed. Over the years, our unit had become one of the top-rated National Guard units in the country. The 30th Brigade, as a whole, was quite well known, respected, and held to a high standard equal to the active duty components that were doing those same jobs day-in and day-out.

The esprit de corps associated with the history of our unit, which included the battle of New Orleans during the War of 1812, was both a badge of honor and a challenge to be an effective fighting force. It boosted our leadership to a new level and since 2001, the National Guard and all other types of reserve units have shouldered at least half of the load of sustained combat operations in two wars, as well as countless other duty stations across the globe. We were soon to be on the leading edge of our nation's response to terrorism.

When the unit received the alert that federal activation orders were in process of being drawn up, John had already completed his six-year enlistment contract and had exited the military. I reenlisted, was promoted, and accepted a full-time position at the local armory as the unit Readiness NCO. In my job, I performed all the administrative needs of the commander and the unit personnel, in addition to being the first one to receive and field calls from headquarters during activations. In May 2003, I received a call that the unit was being put on alert and that I needed to let everyone know that activation orders would soon follow and when to report. I was also told to start calling soldiers who had recently gotten out of the unit to see if I could recruit anyone to fill empty positions. My first call was to John. I said to him, "Hey, buddy, want a vacation? Lots of sand where we're heading." It didn't take much; that afternoon John met a recruiting officer at the armory to take his oath and sign papers. He wasn't the only one; there were a number of guys who reenlisted to support their brothers in arms.

Our unit received activation orders for the Iraq deployment in

September 2003, and were expected to report to the armory with all of our gear, ready to go, no later than October 1. We reported to the armories and spent fifteen days doing a review of records, signing our life insurance papers, providing emergency contact information, getting our wills and powers of attorney ready, identifying our dependents, and setting up our entitlements for pay. We were also getting equipment and weapons ready, as well as packing all of our stuff into shipping containers. It was a surreal process, being twenty-four and twenty-five years old, filling out a will and power of attorney, knowing that you're going into imminent danger.

Everybody on our combat team was relocated to Fort Bragg. Over the course of a few weeks in October 2003, the various elements of the 30th Brigade would arrive and occupy the old World War II barracks where we started back in 1996. Thousands of us assembled solemnly, after leaving our families behind, and tried to get our bearings in the weathered buildings that were sagging suspiciously and showing their more than half a century of service to troops just like us. The rumor mill was spinning out stories that our new barracks were about to be demolished, but they were quickly put back into use as we arrived for duty. Falling into the normal Army routine included the following: undergoing physical training every day, running with all two hundred guys in the battery, and getting into the mode of being an active-duty soldier. We went through retraining to prepare us for what we would face in Iraq, including cultural classes on the Arab world, Islam, and the Arabic language. We were in classes on how to react to an IED, which was new training. What do you do when you're in a convoy of vehicles, something explodes, and the first vehicle is disabled? These were tactics and procedures that we had never experienced in our job.

John mans the gunner hatch during training at Ft. Bragg in 2003.

In January 2004, our unit went to Fort Polk, Louisiana, where we did what they call a mission rehearsal exercise. We went onto a mock-up forward operating base (FOB), which was how the bases in Iraq were structured at the time. We slept in a big circus tent. We had a perimeter guard and did missions where we would go out into the mockup town that was filled with actors who were speaking Arabic and wearing Arabic dress.

It was a very interesting time, to say the least. There were people who were enemies in the woods, who we engaged during foot patrols. There were guys that were shooting simulated mortar rounds at our campus. Everything that was happening in Iraq was recreated in Louisiana.

If you think Louisiana is a decent place in the winter because it's located in the South, Fort Polk is not one of those places. We were out on foot patrol in February. Our unit, including John, went out at 3:00 a.m. We laid down on the ground to hide from the enemy for about an hour and a half. When we tried to get up, our uniforms were frozen to the ground. This was our preparation to go to war in the deserts of Iraq? I learned to embrace and poke fun at the sheer irony the life of a soldier brings sometimes.

Bryan Duckett, after some morale-building mud wrestling while at Ft. Polk, LA, before deploying to Iraq

After our unit returned from Louisiana, all of us got one more break with our families before they started scheduling flights out. It's not just getting on a plane and going over. You're part of a group of nine thousand people and everyone's gear has to be moved in a matter of days. Our group was just a small part of a steady stream of records checks, flight manifests, in-processing and out-processing stations, bus rides, delays, briefings, checkpoints, and a whole list of things we've forgotten. It's a whole flurry of activity that's composed of hundreds of thousands of lives in a mixture of uncertainty, homesickness, and thoughts of what awaited us in the desert.

The C-17 we used to fly into Iraq

Truly, brothers in arms

Inside C-17 first leg flight to Iraq

Everybody else got civilian flights, but because the weather had taken a bad turn, our unit was assigned a military jet. We got up at zero-dark-thirty. Our unit got on two buses with our personal stuff and we drove about ten minutes from our barracks to the Green Ramp at Pope Air Force Base, where we would be boarding the plane. That's where all the paratroopers load their planes, so there was tight security there.

Dale stands in Desert Combat Uniform on his last trip home before deploying to Iraq.

Heavy thoughts and silence were experienced by everyone on those buses. Quiet conversations passed and there was much muttering about how we wound up on an Air Force cargo plane instead of a commercial airliner. As we arrived at the checkpoint to enter the Green Ramp, the bus driver clipped the corner of the guard shack! He accidentally ran the bus into the building while the angry Air

Force Security Forces (SFs) watched in disbelief. I wasn't sure what the driver's problem was, but he was foolish enough to keep driving after ripping off an entire corner of the roof. If you didn't know, the Air Force is very particular about the runway. You don't cross a certain line on that runway or you'll have a gun pointed at you. You don't mess with an airplane on an Air Force runway. Thinking this might've been some kind of security threat, the SFs rolled up in multiple cars with their blue lights flashing. They pulled us over, yanked the driver off of the bus, put him in handcuffs, forced him into one of their cars, and drove away. We were sitting in a bus with no driver, just waiting to go to Iraq. The commander was smart enough to ask, "Who has a bus license?" Sure enough, there was someone in our unit who was qualified to drive a Blue Bird bus. The guy divulged his qualification reluctantly, and after much groaning and booing, drove all of us to the airplane. Our flight was the last one out.

CHAPTER 2

Deployment to Iraq

Dale Beatty

It was snowing heavily when we left. They ended up putting us on a C-17, all set up to haul us and a pallet of our gear in the coldest, most uncomfortable airplane ever. No drinks, no snacks, no flight attendant. There was a bucket in the corner of the plane that rounded out our luxury accommodations, which would be our home for the next twenty-plus hours. We walked up the ramp, got in the cargo nets, and powered off into the snow.

The plane needed to refuel, so we had to land in Newfoundland on a runway that was completely covered in ice. From there, it was on to Ramstein, Germany, to change an engine. After that, our unit "entered the theater" when we put our feet on the ground in Kuwait. We stayed in Kuwait for three weeks, getting acclimated to the weather and doing live fire exercises. The adjustment to the heat, dust, and environment took a while. Crude oil is burned for power there, so oil flames and refineries are burning almost twenty-four hours a day in every direction, putting off a smell that you can almost taste after a while and grow to dislike. This was the least of the unpleasant smells and ambiances of Kuwait.

Finally, our unit moved to a location called The Berm, which is where you cross over from Kuwait into Iraq. We linked up with other units and started heading into Iraq on military convoy routes with other American, British, and Australian convoys.

*Soldiers of Charlie Battery endure the first leg of travel to Iraq
on a military cargo plane after leaving from Ft. Bragg.*

*John stands ready to leave the base manning the M240B
machine gun in the bed of an unarmored HUMVEE.*

John and other soldiers taking a break after
a first full day of convoying into Iraq.

Each unit drove for five days, stopping at a different base every night to sleep, refuel, and eat. Some days we drove until midnight, or until we made it to the next base. Most of our vehicles had no armor, which was scarcely available at our supply base back in Kuwait. They gave us pre-cut and assembled plywood boxes that were to be filled with sandbags and used as potential protection from a blast or small arms fire. Unfortunately, we heard some talk that all it did was increase the pieces of shrapnel that were produced in an IED blast. The next morning, there were sandbags everywhere on the side of the road in the wake of our convoy. We preferred to lighten the load and pray that losing the weight would give us the speed needed to avoid blasts altogether! After a small traffic jam on the outskirts of Saddam Hussein's hometown of Tikrit, eventually we arrived exhausted, dirty, and hungry at our base in Northern Iraq. Hoping to arrive to hot showers, we settled for bathing with five-gallon water cans the next day.

Dale drinks water after a PT run in Iraq.

K-2 Airfield, the base where we were located, had previously been used as an Iraqi air base. It was later named Forward Operating Base Summerall, a nod to the first commanding general of the 1st Infantry Division, our de facto unit of assignment during this tour to Iraq. This base was located about a hundred miles north of Baghdad, between Mosul and Tikrit—near a town called Baiji—a suspected refuge for insurgents and their activity. There were a couple of airplane hangars, a control tower, a runway, and part of a fence that surrounded about a three-mile area. Two thousand combat troops ranging from armor, to mechanized infantry, to artillery were located there. There were also chemical, finance, and mail support units, as well as a few KBR (Kellogg, Brown, and Root) contractors and, much to our comfort, a group of Green Berets as well. Spartan living conditions and terrible Army chow improved gradually to portable toilets and a nice dining facility. Excluding burning human waste from your daily responsibilities did a lot to improve morale. The food improving was by far one of the most celebrated additions to our lives! Real eggs-over-easy after months of shelf-stable food cooked straight out of a cardboard box was a stark reminder of civilization.

Members of 1st Squad, Second Platoon Charlie Battery pose with the Battery Guidon. Front row from left: SPC Ryan Pennington, SPC Bryan Duckett, SPC David Rimmer, and SPC Gary Medlin. Rear row from left: SGT Dale Beatty, SPC John Gallina, SGT Michael Petzold, SGT Daniel Fortman, and SGT David Howell.

Ever present on the highways of Iraq were civilians. We feared being stuck in our Humvees, sitting in huge traffic jams. The Humvees we were in had no doors or roof, nor was there any armor other than sandbags. It's a pretty bad feeling, being that exposed in a place where you know you're a constant target and something could explode or somebody could take a shot at you at any moment. John and I learned by watching other units to adopt an aggressive posture and drive defensively to stand apart as a hard target, with the hopes an enemy would let us pass by unscathed. In spite of our defensively vulnerable vehicles, we always seemed to get lucky and avoid trouble. It was really no secret why we were there. Maybe to the Iraqi people, we were the same as the ones who came before us. However, our unit was tasked as the Hearts and Minds soldiers, sent in to help heal and repair after the 3rd ID blazed their armored vehicles through Iraq during their Thunder Run on Baghdad in early 2003. The disaster was the ground war, and we came to aid those caught in the middle of it, just as our unit did during the American relief missions. Most of us, being parents and husbands or wives ourselves, felt we were truly there to help the country of Iraq recover from disaster.

Dale is caught passing the time reading
during 3rd shift guard duty in Iraq.

The ground war was over after the regime toppled and the search for Saddam Hussein ensued. Now began the insurgent war that has become the face of modern conflicts. A power vacuum displayed itself as multiple militias and religious clerics claimed jihad against us, and each other. Instead of kicking in doors, we were instructed to sling our rifles across our backs and knock on the door, asking to search. We tried to develop friendships with the local nationals, as they were referred to, in order to gain HUMINT, or human intelligence, information that for years has been considered among the most valuable during military operations.

Unfortunately, the first and second battles of Fallujah raged southeast of us, and showed no signs of diminishing. Mortars and rocket attacks plagued our base on a daily or weekly basis, and we watched numerous times as combat patrols exited the gate only to return with casualties from the adjacent city of Baiji. Periodical duties in our roster included base quick reaction force duty, convoy security and patrols, local community search missions for individuals and contraband, and night shift guard duty that most often showed us the war from a distance, with tracers bouncing through the air and Apache helicopters circling for close air support with their devastating guns and rockets. It was like the Wild West, with a potential threat from every direction. Several times, the battle erupted in alleyways and streets, often engaging guard posts a few hundred yards away. Even mosque towers became a potential threat with their perfectly situated vantage points above the towns. From below your feet, from above, or from around a corner in an alleyway or window, the echoes of battle raged in our minds even during the still hours of the graveyard shift. This was war.

A few times, when mortars would sound their telltale thump and I heard screams of "Incoming!" then the bang, crunch, and crash of the impact, I wondered if the next one was headed my way. Supposedly, you were in the wrong spot if you heard it whistling. Rockets were a bit different in that you heard nothing until they were screeching in.

*John and Sgt McCormick [a Vietnam veteran], and PFC Gary Medlin
pose for an Independence Day photo at FOB Summerall.*

*Dale grills up some steaks on a makeshift grill at
FOB Summerall on the 4th of July in Iraq.*

Members of Charlie Battery relax by playing computer games at FOB Summerall in Iraq. Left to right seated Gary Medlin, Daniel Fortman, Ryan Pennington, Jacob Dunford, Byran Duckett. Standing Mike Parker and Patrick Tobin.

November 15, 2004

It was November 2004, and the end of our tour was approaching. John and I settled into a routine of life in combat, whatever that might be. By this time, everybody is tired, irritable, and ready to go home. The endless nights and days are somewhat of a distant memory, but we will remember the imminent dangers and brutal, unforgiving heat forever.

Ryan Pennington, Bryan Duckett (my driver), and I were all trained as combat lifesavers (CLS), which is basically a common soldier who's had at least one opportunity to prove that he can start an IV bag filled with saline successfully with a catheter into a classmate's arm. In the absence of a true medic, the CLS becomes a first responder in a medical situation. Trained to treat wounds, stop bleeding, and introduce fluids right away, CLS personnel have saved countless lives with treatment during the golden hour after injuries are sustained. I signed up half of my squad to attend this mission. Ryan's first responder experience and medical training, at his advanced level, would later prove to be the difference between life and death for me.

We received a mission briefing that arrived late in the afternoon on November 14. They put the mission together and I received the orders around 10:00 p.m. This mission, which would kick off at first light, was to provide security for an engineer group that was sweeping a road that was mined heavily with IEDs. There had been thirty explosions on this road over the last twenty-eight days. This road was important because it served as an alternative supply route for fuel that was going to the second battle of Fallujah.

As my primary driver, Bryan would be there just like he had been every other day during this grueling tour. Having two young kids at home seemed to be taking its toll on Bryan. He was a bit younger than me, and I kind of took him under my wing; we were all but inseparable, as drivers and assigned leaders are often apt to be. I informed the rest of the squad that we had a new truck as I tossed Bryan the keys. I said to everyone, "OK, the DIVARTY Commander is redeploying, and we got his brand new up-armored Humvee. Go down to their motor pool and get it."

A typical M114 up-armored HUMVEE similar to the one driven on November 15, 2004.

Outlaw 21 just about to start a convoy
security mission leaving FOB Summerall.

There was some grumbling between Bryan and John about who would be first to move. They were the ones who had to do the extra work to get ready, after all. I think Bryan even asked if it could wait until we returned from the mission. After four and a half hours at a meeting for the mission, I got irritated and told them to just shut up and get it done. I then took off my boots and got in my rack to study the route and get some sleep, using my sergeant's prerogative. It was around 11:00 p.m. and they were already in their beds getting ready to sleep, so I understood their resentment. However, we were upgrading from a Pinto to a Cadillac and after briefing, we needed and wanted that armored vehicle!

An Improvised Explosive Device [IED]
discovered by Charlie Battery while on patrol.

It took us several hours to transfer all of our equipment from our old truck into the new one. They had to upload encryption data for what's called the Blue Force Tracker, a GPS system that shows where all the units are located on the battlefield. They also had to prepare the weapons systems and check out the vehicle to make sure it was roadworthy for a mission in desert conditions.

At about 4:30 a.m., we left on our mission to patrol the route. John was in the gunner hatch.

John, after returning from a mission, holds
a rocket discovered during a house search.

Bryan was driving. I was in the passenger seat. Having waited for the engineers way past the start time, the decision was finally made to continue the mission after being unable to contact the unit we were supposed to escort. We drove all the way to the end of the route through a very rural area, seeing nothing but a few houses, some shepherds, and an old train loading station that obviously had been in disuse for sometime. Bryan and John were both struggling to stay vigilant. To help him stay awake, Bryan suggested that he and John swap positions, something they did frequently since we were all cross-trained for each job and function on the team. I approved, so John took the driver's position and Bryan jumped up into the gunner hatch. The gunner hatch has more air circulation, but the sun is directly on you and it just bakes you. In the driver's seat, the sun is not directly on you, but the windows are up and there's no air circulation. At around 10:00 a.m., we turned around, backtracking our route, and we stopped just a few miles up the road and set up a hasty traffic control point, which was one of the mission objectives. We searched maybe half a dozen cars or so and received the order to mount up and continue the patrol.

We were the last vehicle in the convoy. Four other vehicles, two of which had no armor, were in front of us, each just as vulnerable and susceptible to the dangers that laid ahead. Each vehicle was separated by about half of a football field, which was standard protocol for us when not in urban areas. Everyone was groggy and I tried to interject some humor, so I pulled out my camera and started recording a short video. I said, "There's Dougie (John's nickname)," and then, "There's Sergeant Cologne," who was from another unit but was riding with us. Then, I looked up at Bryan and said, "There's Duckett." I turned around and shut the camera off. Looking back at the video, just as I was finishing, I could see a large rock on the side of the route that had "This Way to Hell," painted on it, with an arrow pointing in the direction we were traveling. That certainly dampened the mood.

We had received a warning earlier that the insurgents were placing explosives in old potholes and patching them up with fresh asphalt to make them look like a road crew had been there. People drove over it with confidence because it's brand new asphalt. That was the deception that had surely resulted in some of the reported explosions on this route.

*A second landmine discovered on November 16th on
the same site of John, Dale, and Bryan's injuries.*

Remembering the tactic, I saw one of those freshly patched potholes in the middle of the road just as we were passing the tall rock with graffiti. I said, "John, go around that. Do you see that?" John replied, "Yeah. Yeah, I see that." We then proceeded to steer around the pothole instead of straddling it like the vehicle directly in front of us did. As the right front tire got off the road and went into the gravel shoulder, in that brief moment, the mines hidden in the gravel on the side of the road detonated. The explosion lifted the nearly two and half ton Humvee, flipping it end-over-end, landing it facing the reverse direction.

The crater formed by the landmine blast on November 15, 2004, with Bryan being treated in the background.

Within seconds, we were upside down, unconscious, and severely injured. I was blown out of the rear passenger door of the Humvee, seat and all. Every bolt and weld on the vehicle was broken. The Humvee was positioned mostly on its side, but precariously close to tipping over. The only thing that kept it from completely rolling over onto me was the gunner shield and the trunk lid that had popped open. Bryan was ejected through the gunner hatch on the roof, landing a good distance away. Sergeant Cologne was thrown out of the vehicle as well, and it's a mystery as to how he made it out with minimal injury. However, John was still in the vehicle.

November 15th, 2004. A photo is snapped mere moments after the landmine explosion. Ryan Pennington and another medic can be seen treating Dale's wounds in the vehicle to the left with others treating John just beyond the destroyed Humvee.

Soldiers prepare to recover the destroyed HUMVEE at the scene on November 15, 2004.

Ryan, who was also in our squad, was driving the Humvee in front of us and saw the explosion in his rearview mirror. He stopped the truck immediately, jumped out, grabbed his medic bag from the back, and ran straight to our Humvee to help us. He looked through the vehicle and saw John lying on the passenger side roof in a pool of blood, unconscious. He looked over at me and immediately noted the severity of the situation, and that I was awake and aware of what was happening. I was lying in a puddle of diesel fuel with one of my boots just in front of my knee. My entire right leg was severed and twisted around in an unnatural way. My face had been flash-burned and was covered in shrapnel from the blast, but I was alive and talking, so Ryan worked quickly to keep me as such. During those first few minutes, others from our convoy came to our aid. As Ryan was tending to me, Mike Parker, Ken Church, and other combat lifesavers came to our aid. Mike dragged John out of the

Humvee and moved him away from it, closer to where Bryan was being treated for his injuries.

Ryan placed a tourniquet on my right leg. He hooked me up to an IV, as Mike helped put me on a stretcher, and moved me onto another Humvee that had arrived with a medic in a passing convoy. Ryan cut off my other boot and realized that I needed a tourniquet for that leg as well. I was losing a substantial amount of blood. The forty-five-minute wait for the helicopter felt like an eternity to everyone on the scene. Once a helicopter arrived, I was secured inside and taken away to the medical station at FOB Speicher.

The remains of the up-armored HUMVEE that Dale, John, and Bryan were in on November 15, 2004.

John and Bryan get their first look at the destroyed HUMVEE after returning from the hospital.

John was essentially unconscious the entire time, with a serious head wound and his face completely matted with blood. The guys who were tending to him wouldn't give him any water, because drinking water can induce shock. There was no doubt that he was already in shock. After he screamed some vulgarities, fearful of not being able to see, and not knowing where everyone was, they finally decided to help him rinse his face with some water. He was bleeding from his arm, leg, and head, but they said that he wasn't concerned with any of that—he was just concerned about me. John kept asking over and over again, "Where's Dale?" No one would tell him how I was, nor would they let John see me. It wasn't until after my right foot had been amputated, and the ER doctor came to see John and Bryan in another area of the hospital where they were being treated, that they would learn the severity of my injuries.

After I was taken away in the helicopter, another helicopter landed within five minutes to get John and Bryan. As they were led toward the helicopter, the dust-off medic realized that John had gone into shock. All John could hear was ringing. If somebody tried to talk, they had to be touching—like, foreheads touching—so that John could hear what they were saying. They told John to put on his helmet and as he did, it made him feel very nauseated. He removed it quickly, not wanting to be a bad passenger, and used his helmet to vomit in and then, being completely delirious, John put the helmet back on his head. The medic laughed and made John lay down on the stretcher while he proceeded to clean him up.

Bryan broke one of his arms and a disc in his back. His shoulder ligaments were messed up pretty badly. The other guy, the sergeant who was with us, had such minor injuries that he returned to the base with the unit without being medically evacuated. Someone later recalled, "He was running around on adrenaline, ready to fight. He was alert and ready to shoot somebody. Later on, we found out that every time he would leave his base, the convoy he traveled in would get hit." In response, I said, "Asking someone how many times they've been blown up is now a prerequisite to ride with us."

Looking back on the situation is interesting. People say that hindsight is 20/20, however, there were five Humvees in that convoy, and we were the last vehicle. Everybody else drove past that landmine, while driving over the visible perceived threat. We swerved to avoid what we thought could be a potential hazard and drove right into another hazard. You would think that the first vehicle would be the one to hit it, but it's not always that way. Contrasted with the decision to accept the armored Humvee just hours before, it seems more about destiny and less about looking back for lessons learned.

Coming Home

On the same day of the explosion, I had my right leg amputated. I was also intubated for inhalation damage. The next day, they transported me to Landstuhl, Germany, where I stayed for a day and a half. On November 19, 2004, I was admitted into Walter Reed Army Medical Center in Washington, DC.

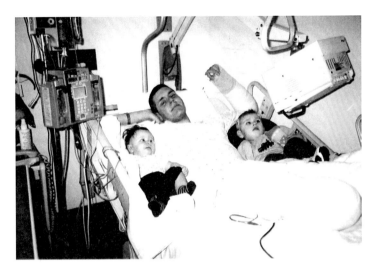

Dale, at Walter Reed Army Medical Center with his sons, Dustin, 2 [R] and Lucas, 6 months old [L]

Dale and his family receive from Chairman of Joint Chiefs General Meyers and his wife.

I was an inpatient for approximately thirty days. During that time, I met all types of people, got incredibly sick, and had several surgeries. I ended up having my left leg amputated as well. I received my Purple Heart from President George W. Bush and was introduced to the Fisher House, which is essentially a home away from home for military families that have extended hospital stays. My family ended up getting a room with them. Eventually, after becoming an outpatient, I joined them at the Fisher House, learning the true value of family medicine.

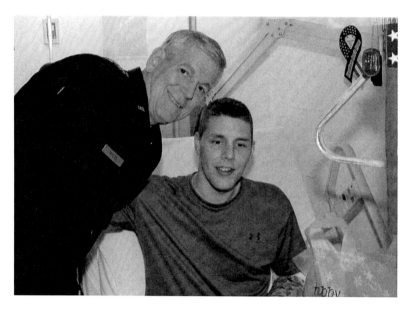

Dale, at Walter Reed Army Medical Center with General Meyers

In February 2005, as soon as John, Ryan, and Bryan landed in the States, they were given a weekend pass. Their families were waiting eagerly to meet them at the on-post gymnasium at Fort Bragg, where they hugged, kissed, and had dinner, but they all were focused on visiting me. The next morning, they all got up and immediately left for Walter Reed. Reports were few and far between since the explosion and they had all returned to duty, where they continued supporting convoy operations for the Division movement to rotate out of country.

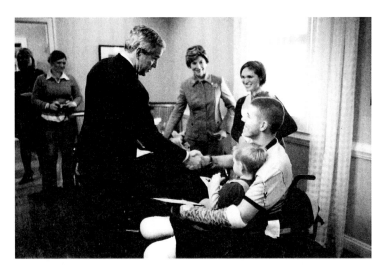

Dale receives a handshake and his Purple Heart medal from President George W. Bush, while his son, Dustin, sits on his lap. Dale's wife, Belinda, along with First Lady Laura Bush smile with admiration and gratitude.

I stayed at Walter Reed for a year. After many surgeries, I learned how to use prosthetics, and then returned home at the end of 2005. However, there were no ramps, elevators, wide doorways, or roll-in showers in my home, as there had been at Fisher House and the hospital. Life as an amputee presented new challenges every day after I moved back home, nearly a year and a half after the injury.

*Dale visits with 6 month old son, Lucas, for the
first time since Lucas' birth just days after injury.*

CHAPTER 3

Life After War

John Gallina

John, en route to Kuwait during his two week leave.

John and Bryan stand in front of the Persian Gulf near the end of tour.

John, Cori-Anne, and their daughter, Jordan, at Charlotte
airport as John is first returning home from Iraq in 2005

John and Jordan after Iraq on his first day home

Shortly after my deployment was completed, along with my contract, my only mission was to go home. However, it took some time before I could actually get comfortable in my own home again. It goes without saying that driving was a challenge for a while. In fact, it took a long time even before I could simply drive to the grocery store. Social interactions became difficult when people I knew would say things to me such as, "You look different" or "Something seems off about you." How are questions like that supposed to make someone feel? I learned quickly that people couldn't understand the experience I had just returned from and it was frustrating for me to try to explain anything about the experience.

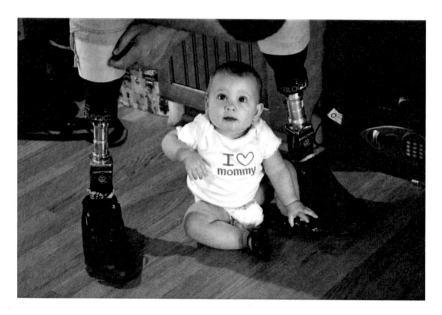

Dale's daughter, Sophia, sitting between Dale's legs while learning how to walk

Preparing for the day

Sure, I was different in some ways after I served in the military. How can someone not be at least somewhat different after going through the experiences I survived? Granted, there is an important perspective that needs to be applied whenever these realizations manifest. Experiences don't define someone. It's the way in which someone uses their experiences to impact others that is most valuable.

John and Cori-Anne attend a Patriot Gala in
Charlotte, NC, to raise funds for charity

Within six months of returning from Iraq, life changed even more for me. I got married and moved to a lovely, picturesque neighborhood in Greensboro, North Carolina. I then resumed working as a building contractor. That's all that I did before in my civilian career, so to me, it made sense to keep doing that type of work. The first job I ended up with was working for a family friend—what a blessing to have him take me under his wing and help me find my way. This working arrangement certainly had its ups and downs (especially when I accidentally shot my own hand with a nail gun), but in the end, I didn't feel as though I was leaving an impact. I felt like I was just working to work, and I wanted to do something greater.

One day, after noticing an impressive-looking construction worker at a gas station, I went up to him and asked if he was hiring. The man said, "I'm always looking for good people." Soon after, I sent this man my resume. Within a few weeks, the man called. I interviewed and got hired. This new job entailed working on very high-end custom homes. My employer was very supportive and kind to me, due to the fact that I was a veteran, and this greatly helped rebuild my self-confidence.

But after a couple of years of continuing to be unsatisfied with my work and having a multitude of diagnoses from the VA—TBI, PTSD, insomnia, post-concussive headaches, and a variety of pills—things were coming to a head. I realized that I didn't see eye-to-eye with my employer and slowly grew to dislike the clientele I was serving as well. The entitlement and perfectionistic mentality of the people I worked for really started to bother me. I couldn't help but remember what the living conditions were like in Iraq, and seeing the little regard these clients showed for fellow Americans (the very people building their homes) struck a chord. I found myself facing a strong internal conflict, yet again questioning what kind of impact I was having. Who was I? Was I really just damaged goods?

I asked my wife, "Maybe I just need a change?" My wife agreed that another change was worth a shot, so I began working for a different company where I was further removed from the clientele and my wife and I moved yet again. Unfortunately, I found that this new company didn't carry a positive culture either. The staff belittled the subcontractors and took advantage of them financially. The military influence of taking care of one another and focusing on the mission still resonated heavily with me. I was still feeling conflicted and searching for a means to use my talents.

During this period of job changes, and about a year after returning home, Dale started looking at building his own house. He and his wife had one child prior to the deployment and were blessed with another six months into our tour in Iraq. I knew that Dale was going to need an accessible house to live in, and we spent hours discussing the different aspects of design, such as accessibility, sustainability, and maintenance impacts. Eventually word got around to Dale's local church and Iredell County Home Builders Association. They all wanted to help with the construction of the house. Dale agreed to accept the help, and the process of building a home for him and his family was underway. As the plans were drawn up, more partners joined, and in the end more than half the materials and labor were donated.

Beatty family home being built with volunteers from the Iredell County Home Builders and local community

A completion party took place after Dale's home was finished. I was running late due to my commute from Greensboro, but was determined to not miss it. Dale was so proud and felt accomplished as he, too, struggled to answer his own questions like, "How can I provide for my family? What are these two little boys going to learn from me?" Dale gained great comfort working beside his father (his lead superintendent) and meeting everyone in the community that poured out love and generous support. It was only natural that after the party ended, I stayed for a while and we discussed what a great outpouring of support he and his family had received. To this day, we continue to experienced endless acts of kindness from the neighbors and entire local area, and these actions made us want to give back. After his home celebration, we began to ask each other, What makes Iraq veterans so special? What about our uncles, great-uncles, and grandfathers? How can we equalize the playing field so that veterans of all eras can receive the same level of care? Both of us saw the opportunity to act on the knowledge that simply because we're disabled veterans, we're not broken. We were tired of hearing things such as, "You have PTSD or a TBI, so you need to sit out." Looking at the older veterans around us, we saw that life doesn't end and injury doesn't have to define you.

Everyone has different struggles. Focusing on helping other people from a positive lens helps you move away from focusing on your own problems. We had a deep desire to help veterans who didn't have the same positive support system that we received after returning from war. We believed strongly that every veteran needs a positive home base in order to proceed with receiving other means of support.

J.J. O'Shea, founder of M1's for Vets, assists Dale in loading his M1 for the first time.

But we had several questions that needed to be answered in order to move forward with our ideas and align our goals: How do we provide a safe haven? How do we encourage others to seek out what they want to do and apply it in a manner that allows them to engage with the community? How can children, college students, adults, and senior citizens get involved? Answers to these questions would develop over time.

I moved back to the Statesville area shortly after Dale's house was completed. At that point, the year was 2008, and the market crashed. The company I worked for closed their doors due to a lack of work.

Dale and John pose for a photo to be sent to Daughters of American Revolution in 2010

At that point, I knew just what needed to be done. I called Dale and said to him, "We've got an opportunity. There's a great gap in the market for charities that are helping older veterans."

We conceptualized and started our nonprofit, Purple Heart Homes, from that conversation.

The Beatty family at home in North Carolina in 2017.
From left: Sophia, Dale, Dustin, Belinda, and Lucas

CHAPTER 4

Different Wars, Different Homecomings

Dale Beatty

THE SAME CANTEEN
by Private Miles O'Reilly

There are bonds of all sorts in this world of ours,
Fetters of friendship and ties of flowers,
And true lover's knots, I ween;
The girl and the boy are bound by a kiss,
But there's never a bond, old friend, like this,
We have drank from the same Canteen!

It was sometimes water, and sometimes milk,
And sometimes applejack "fine as silk;"
But whatever the tipple has been
We shared it together in bane or bliss,
And I warm to you, friend, when I think of this,
We drank from the same Canteen!

The rich and great sit down to dine,
They quaff to each other in sparkling wine,
From glasses of crystal and green;
But I guess in their golden potations they miss

The warmth of regard to be found in this,
We drank from the same Canteen!

We have shared our blankets and tents together,
And have marched and fought in all kinds of weather,
And hungry and full we have been;
Had days of battle and days of rest,
But this memory I cling to and love the best,
We drank from the same Canteen!

For when wounded I lay on the center slope,
With my blood flowing fast and so little hope
Upon which my faint spirit could lean;
Oh! then I remember you crawled to my side,
And bleeding so fast it seemed both must have died,
We drank from the same Canteen!

Eventually, a soldier's wartime service ends, and the veteran comes home. However, homecoming isn't always positive. Sometimes, there are no parades. Sometimes, there's no one to greet the returning warrior. It all depends on the politics of the time, the popularity of the war, the veteran's family and friends, his or her injuries, and more. Every veteran's homecoming is different.

The first war in the history of the United States was the Revolutionary War, which involved over 215,000 servicemembers and approximately 4,500 deaths. The Civil War was America's bloodiest war, raging from 1861 until 1865. Counting those on both sides, more than three million took part in that fight, with more than 620,000 deaths from combat, accident, starvation, and disease. This war was followed by the Spanish American War in 1898, in which approximately 300,000 served, with about 2,500 killed. In 1917, World War I began, and more than four million Americans joined the battle. More than 100,000 lost their lives. While there are many other wars that we have not mentioned, no veterans from any of those earlier conflicts are still alive. Today, Purple Heart Homes serves veterans from the wars described below.

World War II: The Greatest Generation

When Pearl Harbor was bombed in December 1941, the nation found itself at war with Japan, and a patriotic fervor swept the land. Soon, a second front opened in Europe, and more than sixteen million men and women—more than 10 percent of the country's population at the time—enlisted or had been drafted to serve until the war ended in 1945.

The entire country was united behind the war effort. Women went to work in factories building airplanes, tanks, and other armaments. Families bought war bonds and planted victory gardens so that food could be grown for the troops. Companies stopped manufacturing automobiles so that steel and rubber could be used for the machines and other necessities of war.

By the end of the war, 291,557 soldiers had been killed in battle and another 113,842 died by other means while in service. 670,846 had sustained non-mortal injuries. Those who returned home were greeted with raucous victory parades and honored by a grateful nation. Even though many of them suffered from post-traumatic stress and other injuries, they found support and opportunities in a booming postwar economy. Veterans were given preference for jobs, and government programs were created to send them to college and help them buy homes. The years after the World War II were some of America's most prosperous, full of achievement and progress.

According to the Department of Veterans Affairs, around 620,000 American veterans from World War II were estimated to still be alive in 2016. But the nation is losing almost five hundred of these veterans each day, and it's estimated that the last one will have died by 2036. Still, the survivors' needs are great, and the community must continue to offer them help.

Korea: The Forgotten War

Most people think of the years after World War II as an era of prosperity and good times, but the anxieties and fear brought on by the start of the Cold War with the Soviets lay just under the surface. There were stories of UFOs in the newspapers, people built bomb shelters in their backyards, and children practiced duck-and-cover exercises under their desks in air raid drills at school. Americans were frightened at the prospect of Communism.

Just a few years after World War II ended, US troops were on the ground in Korea. Though it's referred to as The Forgotten War, Americans didn't so much forget about the Korean War as they never thought about it at all in the first place. It wasn't until 1958 that the conflict in Korea was officially dignified by the term "war." Even today, the Truman Administration's euphemisms "conflict" and "police action" are often used to describe this war. In diplomat W. Averell Harriman's words, Korea was considered a "sour little war." Korea was the first of what we would refer to as a more political war on the homefront. There was opposition to helping the people involved. Americans stood to gain nothing, per se. We weren't being oppressed, it wasn't our freedoms at risk. Why should we involve ourselves?

When Communists took control of China in 1949, President Harry Truman feared that nearby countries such as Korea and Japan would convert as well. Korea had been part of the Japanese Empire. When Japan fell, the United States and Soviet Union agreed to split Korea into two states: North and South. These two states were divided along the 38th parallel. Armed with Soviet rifles and tanks, North Korean troops crossed the 38th parallel on June 25, 1950, and the war was underway.

Coming so soon on the heels of World War II, there were fears that the United States would return to the same type of rationing and full mobilization as it had during the war that had just ended. There were also the millions of families still mourning loved ones, and as a whole, the nation didn't really have the stomach for another war. When that fear didn't come to pass, most people returned back to their own lives and tried to ignore the raging conflict as best as they could.

Approximately 5.7 million military personnel served in Korea between 1950 and 1953. At this point, America now had a standing army that was going into its third major conflict. 33,739 were killed in battle, with another 2,835 deaths from other causes. 103,284 were wounded. About a quarter of the veterans who served in World War II also served in Korea, and many of the veterans who served in Korea went on to serve later in Vietnam. Most of the veterans who fought in Korea served willingly; only one-third were draftees, while the rest enlisted.

The war raged on until 1953, and didn't end in victory for either side. Instead, there was a ceasefire, which is still in effect today. There were no celebrations when the war came to its inconclusive end. In January 1953, the *Army Times* editorialized: "[Korea] is the most 'forgotten war,' and the men who fought in it are lonesome symbols of a nation too busy or too economy-minded to say thanks in a proper manner." Author and *Parade* columnist James Brady remembered, "They didn't stage any parades for us. Then again, people didn't spit at us neither." One former Marine recalled, "Your family welcomed you and that was it. I never talked about the war. People weren't interested and wouldn't know where it was even if you told them."

A distinguishing characteristic of Korean War veterans is their silence. While veterans of both World War II and Vietnam talked about what they did overseas and formed veteran organizations, the veterans who served in Korea mostly came home and tried to pick up their old lives. In some ways, it seems as though the American public subconsciously blamed the war's unsatisfactory outcome on the soldiers who fought there, and the soldiers came home to a stigma attached to a war gone awry. Although most people think that these veterans re-adjusted to civilian life relatively smoothly, no studies were conducted on the psychological impact of a non-supportive society on its citizen soldiers.

The Department of Veterans Affairs estimates that there are about 1.6 million Korean War veterans still alive. Most are in their seventies and eighties, and need benefits appropriate for their age. Cuts in Medicare, Medicaid, affordable housing programs, and food programs all impact them severely.

Vietnam: Demoralizing Guerilla War

Shortly after the Korean stalemate, the United States became engaged in another proxy war against Communism. In 1954, Viet Minh forces won the Battle of Dien Bien Phu and ended French involvement in Indochina. The French and Viet Minh negotiated a ceasefire at the Geneva Conference, with France agreeing to withdraw its troops from the region while Vietnam was divided temporarily at the 17th parallel into North and South Vietnam. General elections were to be held by 1958 to unify the country once more.

The United States feared that the elections would be under the Communists' influence, and if they won in Vietnam, Communism could spread throughout Southeast Asia. American aid to South Vietnam began in January 1955 in support of the administration of Prime Minister Ngo Dinh Diem. The repressive government under Diem resulted in the arrests of more than 25,000 activists. The government also attacked the Buddhist community, and became more and more unpopular among the South Vietnamese. Diem's politics and failed attempts to win favor with the South led to his assassination in 1963.

Another assassination took place in 1963, that of President John F. Kennedy. His successor, Lyndon B. Johnson, stated in late November of that year, "Strength and determination must be used in the battle against Communism," and confirmed his intention to continue American military and economic support to South Vietnam.

On August 2, 1964, the US destroyer *Maddox* exchanged fire with North Vietnamese torpedo boats in the Gulf of Tonkin, and reported coming under fire again two days later. Most historians, including those in the US military, have since concluded that the second attack never took place. Still, the incident served as a pretext for a massive buildup of the war. Johnson ordered airstrikes by the end of the day, and by March 1965, 3,500 US Marines were sent to South Vietnam, marking the start of ground war there. By the end of that year, more than 180,000 American troops were in Vietnam, with more on the way.

These troops, some of whom were draftees, found themselves in a different kind of war, fighting against a sometimes-invisible enemy, who often intermingled and blackmailed the civilian population. It was here in Vietnam where, despite there still being a marked battle line, the overall tactics of general warfare drifted further and further from past types of warfare. America would see more of those changes through the Vietnam War and into an urban type of guerilla warfare in Iraq. Our fighters were constantly on edge. Morale was often low, and drugs ranging from marijuana to heroin were readily available to help them escape the realities surrounding them.

Meanwhile, back at home, the situation was turning ugly. Television news reports brought the brutality of the war into the nation's living rooms. The steady increase in combat casualties eroded civilian support. Deaths surged from 1,928 in 1965 to 16,998—more than forty-five killed each day—by 1968. Protests against the war began to escalate, and college campuses were rife with demonstrations, teach-ins, sit-ins, occupied buildings, draft card burnings, and other disruptions. The war affected US politics at the highest levels, giving rise to popular anti-war candidates, which finally led to Johnson's decision not to run for reelection in 1968. What started off as a good faith effort to help an oppressed people and negotiate peace ended up with the shedding of American blood. The media, one of the only sources of information for those at home, was flooded with reports of high death tolls and perceived American defeat.

When Richard Nixon took office in January 1969, he recognized that his mandate was to end the war in Vietnam. Nixon didn't want to be accused of losing, so he set out to forge an agreement with the enemy to buy time while placating the American public with token troop withdrawals. By the spring of 1970, there were 150,000 fewer American troops in Vietnam than there had been in the year prior. Two years later, the number of troops, once nearly half a million, had fallen to 65,000. This low number undermined the South Vietnamese regime's security. Meanwhile, at the negotiation table, Henry Kissinger, Nixon's national security advisor, made an agreement that Northern troops could remain in the South after a settlement, essentially selling out our allies. The war dragged on, with a disillusioned Congress appropriating fewer resources each year. In April 1975, the North Vietnamese overthrew Saigon and renamed it Ho Chi Minh City, after their revolutionary leader. The largest helicopter evacuation in history took place as American civilian and military personnel, along with tens of thousands of South Vietnamese civilians who had cooperated with the regime, were flown out of the country. It was perceived as a humiliating defeat for the United States.

Veterans returning home to this politically charged climate were often not received kindly. There were no parades for them. They weren't just ignored, like the veterans returning from Korea. They were also singled out, scapegoated, called "baby killers," spat upon, discriminated against for jobs, and ostracized. Some veterans were bitter, seeking solace in drugs and alcohol, and some fell into homelessness. This took place even before they began to realize the delayed effects of Agent Orange that would lead to diabetes and other complications.

Our Vietnam veterans experienced a much different type of warfare. They fought in a guerilla war, whereas the soldiers of World War II fought in a Napoleonic war that still had lines of battle. The guerilla tactics utilized in Vietnam were demoralizing. The results of their actions and abilities were picked on and looked down upon by the American public. They were not viewed as great leaders and great men. Consequently, this created a deeper, moral injury that has plagued this generation of veterans.

Thousands of Vietnam veterans returned home unaware that they had been exposed to toxic dioxin that was intended to combat the vegetation giving cover to the Viet Cong guerrillas and the North Vietnamese Army. An estimated 20 million gallons were sprayed over much of Vietnam in an attempt to uncover roads and trails used by the enemy. Today, decades later, Agent Orange is catching up with these veterans and bringing with it deadly health problems such as cancer and heart disease.

One veteran, Dave Morrell, became a severe diabetic due to his exposure. He told me, "I started showing signs when I was twenty-six years old. Now, I'm sixty-four, and I'm taking seven insulin shots a day. I can't feel my feet anymore." Other symptoms veterans experience are high blood pressure and irregular heartbeat, let alone post-traumatic stress.

Congress didn't pass the Agent Orange Act, giving the Department of Veterans Affairs power to declare certain health conditions as presumptive to dioxin exposure, until 1991—long after the war ended. However, the Department of Veteran Affairs doesn't have an accurate count of how many Vietnam veterans suffer from exposure to Agent Orange. Local Disabled American Veteran chapters help Vietnam veterans find the medical and financial coverage for their illnesses associated with Agent Orange by aiding veterans in filling out their disability claims to the Department of Veteran Affairs, revealing a greater, unspoken need for housing modifications and community support.

The First Gulf War: Desert Storm/Desert Shield

When Saddam Hussein's Iraqi army invaded Kuwait on August 2, 1990, there were several reasons for doing so. They accused Kuwait of stealing Iraqi petroleum through slant drilling, which proved to be one of the primary reasons for the invasion. Another prominent reason was that they were unhappy with Kuwait's large production of oil, which kept revenues down for Iraq. After two days of intense combat, the Iraqi Republican Guard overran the Kuwaitis, and many of Kuwait's Armed Forces fell back into neighboring Bahrain and Saudi Arabia. Saddam Hussein announced that the Emirate of Kuwait was now annexed and would become the 19th province of Iraq.

One month before the invasion, April Glaspie, the US ambassador to Iraq, questioned the Iraqi high command about the military preparations in progress and the massing of troops near the Kuwaiti border. She advised that the United States had no opinion on Arab-Arab conflicts, and that Washington didn't intend to start an economic war against Iraq. Hussein came away believing that he had received a diplomatic O.K. to invade Kuwait. The US government thought that Hussein was interested only in pressuring the Kuwaitis into lowering their oil production and forgiving some of the debt Iraq had incurred for the recently concluded Iraq-Iran war. This misunderstanding had grave consequences.

Iraq's invasion and occupation of Kuwait was condemned by all major world powers, even some of Iraq's closest allies. Several countries set up arms embargoes, and by the end of 1990, the United States had demanded that Iraq withdraw its forces or face war. Negotiations failed, and the US-led coalition forces and launched a military assault on Iraq in mid-January 1991. Allied aircraft destroyed the Iraqi Air Force, along with several other Iraqi military sites. The war looked as though it would be over almost as soon as it had begun.

As the Iraqis began to retreat, they retaliated by igniting over six hundred Kuwaiti oil and natural gas wells, refineries, and storage tanks, creating lakes of oil in low-lying areas and filling trenches. The smoke and fire that hung over the desert could be seen in satellite photos from space for months, and is etched forever into the memory of those whom served. One veteran, Scott Emory, reported, "It was like a cloudy day all day long. In fact, we didn't realize it was smoke at first. The smoke was about five hundred feet above us, so we couldn't see the sky. However, we could see horizontally for long distances with no problem. We knew it was smoke when the mucous from our nostrils started to look black."

Fighting continued until February 25, when Kuwait was liberated from Iraq. The quick victory was regarded as one of the greatest military achievements of all time, and the returning veterans were seen as heroes. Just seventeen years after the humiliating experience of the loss of the Vietnam War, the United States had its military mojo back. It was a triumph for the first war fought by an all-volunteer force. President George H.W. Bush declared a New World Order with the United States as the most powerful country in the world, leading a coalition of allies and former enemies, including the Soviet Union.

More than 650,000 service members were deployed to the first

Gulf War, and because the war was over so quickly and fought largely in the air, there were relatively fewer casualties compared to previous wars. Only 148 were killed in battle, with 235 other deaths in the theater. 467 troops were non-mortally wounded. A ticker-tape parade was held in New York City for 200,000 of the returned veterans, led by Bush and General "Stormin' Norman" Schwarzkopf.

The twenty-fifth anniversary of the liberation of Kuwait passed in February 2016, but the Pentagon held no formal observance. After all these years, there are many veterans of that conflict who are experiencing problems now known as Gulf War Syndrome. These include undiagnosed illnesses such as abnormal weight loss, fatigue, cardiovascular disease, joint pain, headache, menstrual disorders, neurological and psychological problems, skin conditions, respiratory disorders, and sleep disturbances. Diagnosable functional gastrointestinal disorders include irritable bowel syndrome, functional dyspepsia, vomiting, constipation, bloating, abdominal pain, and dysphagia. Chronic fatigue syndrome and fibromyalgia are also thought to be part of the syndrome.

There are more than two million living veterans from Desert Storm/Desert Shield, most of whom are now in their fifties.

Today's Wars: Iraq and Afghanistan

The United States invaded Afghanistan after the 9/11 attacks in 2001 in search of Osama bin Laden. The intent was to take out Al-Qaeda and deny them a safe haven by defeating the Taliban. This intention began the longest war in our history, which continues to this day.

It was called Operation Enduring Freedom. Great Britain was one of our principal allies. In 2003, NATO took control of the operation, and called them the International Security Assistance Force (ISAF). Troops from forty-three different countries were represented, though the majority of those who served were Americans. By August 2010, there were over 100,000 US troops in Afghanistan. In July 2016, there were still more than 8,000 there.

The Taliban forces were particularly brutal in waging an asymmetrical war. Guerilla raids and ambushes throughout the countryside were a constant threat, and suicide bombers wreaked havoc on the cities. There were improvised explosive devices and rocket attacks on bases. The Afghan government, one of the most corrupt in the world, was often suspected of supporting the Taliban behind the scenes.

Two years after opening the war in Afghanistan, in March 2003, the United States invaded Iraq, based on questionable intelligence that Saddam Hussein was harboring weapons of mass destruction. American forces began bombing Baghdad, Iraq's capital, shortly after a deadline that had been given to Hussein to leave the country passed without him doing so. Soon thereafter, he went into hiding. The invasion toppled his regime and captured most of the major cities in only three weeks, with very few casualties on the coalition side. In his famous "Mission Accomplished" speech, the President George W. Bush declared an end to major combat hostilities as of May 1, 2003. However, the Iraq war was far from over.

After the collapse of Hussein's government, insurgencies sprung up to fill the power vacuum, and Iraq fell into the chaos of a civil war. Sunnis, who were used to being in control, had treated Shia citizens brutally. At the time, the Shia were running the country, and Nouri al-Maliki, their leader, refused to include Shiites in the government. The rivalry intensified into sectarian violence, or a religious-based civil war. Coalition forces were drawn into the fight, making the occupation of the country difficult. It would take months and many changes in the rules of engagement, but eventually free elections were held in 2004.

Most of the people back home in the United States supported the wars in Afghanistan and Iraq, although there was significant opposition and protest against the Iraq war. Veterans returning home from these deployments have been treated with respect and have been given a lot of support, both by their communities and by the Veterans Administration. More than 2.5 million men and women served in the Army, Navy, Marines, Air Force, Coast Guard, Reserve, and National Guard units since the wars began in Afghanistan in 2001 and in Iraq in 2003. More than one-third were deployed two, three, four or even five times, with just short stays at home between deployments.

A total of 4,491 US service members were killed in Iraq between 2003 and 2014. 32,336 were wounded in action. There have been 2,386 US military deaths in Afghanistan, and 20,049 service members were wounded there. As of 2014, more than 670,000 of the surviving veteran population have been awarded disability status, while another 100,000 applications are still pending.

It remains to be seen whether or not there will be any surprise consequences for the veterans of the wars in Iraq and Afghanistan. What's always been in the back of our minds is what particular version of Agent Orange have John and I been exposed to that's yet to be discovered.

Consider this quote from Von Clausewitz: "War is an extension of politics." Like all wars before us, politics remain in the midst of today's wars. They not only draw us into war, but also divide our nation through them once again.

CHAPTER 5

Moral Injury

John Gallina

Aiai! My name is a lament!
Who would have thought it would fit
so well with my misfortunes!
Now truly I can cry out -- aiai! --
two and three times in my agony.

Aiee, Ajax! My name says what I feel;
who'd have believed that pain and I'd be one;
Aiee, Ajax! I say it twice,
and then again, aiee, for what is happening.

– Sophocles, *Ajax*

On June 7, 2004, a suicide bomber detonated a car bomb at the front gate of our base in Iraq. My squad was on quick reaction force duty. Dale was on leave, home with his wife as she gave birth to their second child. As soon as the bomb went off, I jumped in the truck and headed to the main gate, ready for action. It's not exactly what you might think in many cases, when suicide bombers die and there is often no one to fight. In our case, this suicide bomber used three artillery rounds wired together in the trunk of a BMW to attack our

111

main gate. We immediately set up a perimeter; two members of the squad provided first aid to the injured and others rounded up witnesses for interviews. Each of the members in my squad were affected differently. Dale wasn't there, but knowing that his guys had to go out and put human parts—including those of the bomber—into body bags still haunts him. He wasn't there at a time when he felt he needed to be there.

Horrific, inhuman things happen on the battlefield that cause deep and disturbing injuries. In many cases, these aren't physical injuries. Often, the people who are most injured are those who suffer moral injury. Moral injury is a recent term. It's something that has been identified in the last few years as the root cause of mental disturbances, such as post-traumatic stress triggered by imagery, smells, or sounds that revert an in individual back to the point of trauma or a tragic event.

For many, moral injury develops from the sense of barbarism witnessed on the battlefield. Soldiers see the worst of humanity, the worst of anything that people can do to other people. The casualties in that scenario were civilians. They were waiting to get inside the base to work for just a few American dollars an hour, washing clothes or building a wall, or doing something else to support our operations. There were children from ten years old all the way up to elders who were still able-bodied enough do manual labor. Ryan was greatly affected by this experience. Never would he show up to the scene of an accident back home the same as before, ultimately finding the experience too emotionally difficult to do the simplest of tasks such as CPR. These civilians were all just waiting in line and got killed for being in the wrong place at the wrong time. It's not necessarily the full-out motive, not necessarily the A-team mission, but that's what happens on the battlefield.

*The aftermath of the vehicle borne improvised explosive
device [VBIED] at FOB Summerall in June 2004*

While the term moral injury may be a term interjected recently in
our society, the concept of moral injury is nothing new. Throughout history, warriors, philosophers, and poets have wrestled with the
ethical dilemmas presented by war. Sophocle wrote *Ajax* in the fifth
century BC as a response to the Trojan War. This tragic play portrays

the anguish and eventual suicide of Ajax after his friend Achilles is killed in the war.

Shell shock was a term used to describe a condition found in World War II soldiers who had been in the trenches under artillery bombardment. Exposure to too much concussion can cause traumatic brain injury—a physiological rather than psychological brain injury. These soldiers couldn't move, and were often terrified or physically broken down to the point where all they could do was pace. It went from being called shellshock, to battle fatigue, to combat stress, to post-traumatic stress.

Now, we refer to the psychological injury as *moral injury,* which gives a much deeper connotation and understanding. The term is thought to have originated from the writings of Vietnam War veteran and peace activist Camillo "Mac" Bica.

Morals are developed by society, by family. You're taught what's right and wrong during your upbringing. The Veterans Administration describes it in this way: "Events are considered morally injurious if they transgress deeply held moral beliefs and expectations. Thus, the key precondition for moral injury is an act of transgression, which shatters moral and ethical expectations that are rooted in religious or spiritual beliefs, or culture-based, organizational, and group-based rules about fairness, the value of life, and so forth."

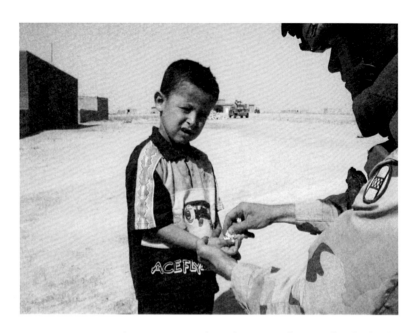

Ryan Pennington shares some candy with an Iraqi boy at a local school.

Consider a soldier in Vietnam, who was brought up by a good family that taught him right from wrong. Willing to serve his country, he had no understanding when he signed up for the war that he would be confronted with babies tied to bombs on the battlefield, booby-trapped so that the baby would be killed as well as the person attempting to save the baby. As a soldier with good morals trying to act humane, he was confronted with killing the child in order to keep from having to hear it cry until it died from the explosion. Imagine his sense of moral transgression.

An Iraqi boy guards the gift of water that 'fell off' the back of our HUMVEE.

*A U.S. Interpreter speaks with an Iraqi farmer holding his daughter
just outside of FOB Summerall during a HUMNIT mission.*

The Viet Cong were placing babies on the battlefield to hide the bombs. Yet when the soldier returned home after the war, he was subjected to propaganda instigating confrontation in America by protesters and others against the veteran for the war he had just fought. The veteran survived the battlefield just to come home and fight both his fellow citizens and his own demons formed from time in a combat zone.

Soldiers of Charlie Battery 2nd platoon stand with teachers and students from a primary school west of FOB Summerall after delivering school supplies, candy, and other requests from home for the children.

Treating Moral Injury

The University of Syracuse formed the Moral Injury Project in 2014 to address the question: *What are we doing about moral injury among US military veterans?* They state, "Returning veterans, and those who care for them, are struggling to understand and respond effectively when experiences of war result in levels of anguish, anger, and alienation not well explained in terms of mental health diagnoses such as post-traumatic stress disorder (PTSD)." They define moral injury as, "disruption in an individual's confidence and expectations about one's own or others' motivation or capacity to behave in a just or ethical manner." They describe moral injury as, "the inability to contextualize or justify personal actions or the actions of others and the unsuccessful accommodation of these… experiences into pre-existing moral schemas." They speak of a "deep soul wound that pierces a person's identity, sense of morality, and relationship to society."

When you have this type of response or regression in your feelings or emotional state, it's not always treated as an injury, but rather as a form of post-traumatic stress. That's how Vietnam veterans have been treated for years, as though they have a disorder, when in actuality they are completely normal. When they went to Veteran Affairs and explained some of their feelings, they were treated as if it were a psychological problem, and often were prescribed medication.

However, pills don't treat a moral injury. Humans help heal that moral injury. Somebody acting compassionately and saying, "I don't understand, but I love you and appreciate you for going and doing what I wasn't willing to do—confronting the evil in the world that I wasn't willing to confront," is a step in the right direction.

Ajax in the Modern Day

In 2009, the Pentagon funded a group called Theater of War, which has staged more than 250 shows for 50,000 military personnel on bases from Europe to Guantanamo. The actors present a modern adaptation of Sophocles' *Ajax* to full houses of soldiers. The play addresses the challenges and feelings that warriors face when they deploy and later return home. After his best friend was killed on the battlefield, Ajax blamed himself and while mourning his loss, wanted Achilles' shield, feeling that somehow it would help him win this battle. Ajax spoke to his general, who wouldn't give him the shield. Later on, when Ajax went home, he was depressed, and, in a fit of rage, destroyed his house and slaughtered hundreds of cattle. He wanted to kill the general and blamed him for everything—particularly his bad decisions in sending them to war.

Many of the soldiers who saw the play included those who had been deployed to combat multiple times in Iraq and Afghanistan, many of whom were still dealing with post-traumatic stress and battle trauma. These soldiers understood Ajax's suicide. Nearly one veteran an hour commits suicide, but that number is often misunderstood. Those suicides are represented by veterans of all generations.

Also, it's important to make a distinction about the number of veterans who commit suicide. The number is proportional to those in the general population in the same age group who end their own lives. However, the message often heard by society—and by veterans themselves—is that the veterans are damaged, and that suicide is a normal response and option for them. It isn't, and we need to change the way we present the need.

Theater of War presents these plays so soldiers can see that these are age-old emotions that they're dealing with and that they're not alone. Understanding that it was not only veterans of the twentieth and twenty-first centuries go through these experiences helps with the coping process. Civilians can relate to them in some ways, but these moral injuries have been inflicted for over four thousand years. Veterans need to understand that they're not misunderstood or broken, and that they can harness their emotions. Then they'll realize that their reactions are normal in order to move forward, do good, and continue being who they are and not be transformed into someone that they don't want to be.

Marine Corps veteran, Manny Jimenez, poses outside of the framing of his new home with volunteers from H.E.A.R.T 9/11 working in the back.

Helping heal those with moral injuries is a large part of what Purple Heart Homes does. For example, Dale and I were working on a project for an Afghanistan veteran in Connecticut. More than one hundred New York firemen came to work, and framed the entire house in just a matter of days. We threw a dinner to thank them for volunteering. One of the volunteers was a Vietnam veteran. He showed up every week, at least three times each week.

The veteran comes up at the dinner and asks, "Can I say a few words?" I said, "Sure, you're a Vietnam vet. You can say whatever you want. I'll hold everybody here for as long as you want to talk." The guy gets up, breaks down in tears, and says, "I've never felt like I was at home. I've never felt like anybody cared about veterans. For forty years, I've held this anger and resentment inside that I've had towards America. I volunteered to go. I volunteered for service, came home, and not only was I not welcomed, but I felt unwelcomed. Seeing all of these volunteers and citizens come together to help this young Afghanistan veteran, it's helped me be able to let go of that anger."

Even the volunteers get something out of the experience. It was eye-opening that these morally injured people just want to be loved and received, and see the great benefit that he received from spending time helping someone like him, but generations apart.

CHAPTER 6

Veterans from Different Conflicts

Dale Beatty and John Gallina

Ryan Pennington

Ryan was born in Southern California. When his father was transferred by his employer during the 1980s, Ryan's family relocated to Lincolnton, North Carolina, not far from where we lived. His father worked as a production manager for a manufacturing company and his mother was a child nutrition director for the local school system. As Ryan grew up, he maintained an interest in joining the military. His grandfather served in World War II, and his father served in Vietnam.

Ryan shares a military heritage with us, starting in the National Guard. He enjoyed the twelve years he spent in the National Guard, especially the time spent in the field away from the normal routine of civilian life. When we asked him why he was so happy during that time, he responded, "It's something different.... especially when you're doing this just thirty-nine days out of the year, you don't get that redundancy. You don't necessarily get tired of it. What other part-time job can you have where you go out into the woods and shoot hundred-pound high explosive rounds?"

Ryan Pennington at dusk just before guard duty at FOB Summerall

In civilian life, Ryan held a full-time job, was a volunteer firefighter, and worked part-time with Cleveland County Emergency Medical Services as a medic and first responder. It was the excitement of the National Guard that he enjoyed so much. He was one of the most upbeat people we served with—always willing to go and do something new, learn all that he could, while lending a helping hand and a friendly smile.

The excitement was definitely something that we both looked forward to as well, although we dreaded it a little bit at the same time. It was like being able to go out every month with some of your best friends. The camaraderie that develops in a National Guard unit is different because sometimes people stay in those units for twenty years. There are both older and younger people in the same unit. The unit becomes a family.

Playing video games during downtime near the end of tour in Iraq.
Left to right: Fortman, Duckett, Petzold, Beatty, and Tobin

Bryan Duckett, after some morale-boosting mud wrestling

Looking at our roster in 2003, it was clear that we didn't have the strength we needed after a couple of replacements washed out due to medical issues. Ryan wound up serving in the same squad where Dale was the squad leader. When asked how he felt about his deployment, Ryan told us, "You sign up with that risk and know that day might come. You just accept it and you go. I wouldn't say I'm frightened and I wouldn't say that I'm excited, but there's an uncertainty. You don't know. You don't know what it's going to be like, what you're going to be put up against. You train a certain way and build your own personality to accept whatever the next day brings. It's a mission. It's a job. It's my own will that accepted this job. It's time to go to work, and that's really the way you need to look at it."

Outlaw 21 beginning a training exercise at Ft. Bragg.
Left to right: John, Ryan, Michael Petzold, and Daniel Fortman

After returning from Walter Reed and visiting Dale, the next hurdle was processing out of the military. Ryan's contract was complete, and he too had been stop-loss for months while continuing to serve in Iraq. After receiving his DD214, he was finally headed home.

He spent his first week just decompressing at the house. The next week, he and his wife went on a Caribbean cruise, all part of Ryan's plan to put Iraq behind him and get back to normal. After they returned from their trip, Ryan stayed home for another week before starting up his civilian job again. He yearned to have a normal life as soon as possible.

Ryan and his daughter, Abby

Abby leading Ryan out of the airport for two weeks of down time

Ryan says he felt as though transitioning back to civilian life was easy. But if you ask around, most people will say the transition back is not easy at all. A year had passed before Ryan realized how his time in Iraq had changed him—and how it changed his loved ones when they lived without him being there. During his two-year absence, Ryan's family figured out how to function without him. Whenever he came around to help with something, he'd say, "Hey, you don't have to do this all the time, I can help." This caused conflict. His family was still moving on the way they had become accustomed to while he was away.

He returned to his old job at the same manufacturing company that his father had retired from, as the environmental health and safety manager. Things were also difficult at work. The company had become accustomed to his absence as well.

It wasn't long before Ryan and his wife began to experience problems in their marriage. Before Iraq, they were always on the go—hanging out with friends, going here and there, doing this and that—but he didn't want that kind of life anymore. The return home came with the realization that he had missed two years of his daughter's life. He didn't want to go anywhere. He didn't want to go out to eat or go to his friends' houses. He just wanted to stay home. His preference was to avoid commotion all together. If he was in a crowd, it felt like hearing nails on a chalkboard. He didn't like a lot of ambient noise. Everything in his life had to be very structured and organized in order for him to feel comfortable. That was one of the big divides in their marriage. His wife still wanted to go out and do things. They couldn't find common ground anymore, and there were control issues that ultimately resulted in their separation.

Nobody tells you how to deal with post-traumatic stress. Ryan started realizing how everyone at home and work had been affected by his absence and life started to unravel quickly. Ryan decided to seek help from Veterans Affairs, and began talking with a psychiatrist once a month. He felt good during his sessions, but he would leave every time with some type of prescription.

Ryan had a prescription for a medicine to help him sleep, and another medicine that was supposed to help with post-traumatic stress. He took the pills and soon realized that they made him feel incoherent and out-of-touch with reality. He felt terrible. After about a year, he stopped taking his medicine. Any time he would receive those pills in the mail, he would pour them in a Ziploc bag of kitty litter and white vinegar, destroy them, and throw them in the trash. In retrospect, Ryan believes that the medications contributed to the troublesome issues he was experiencing in his life.

Soon after the separation from his wife came the divorce, and Ryan's life continued to unravel. Like most fathers, Ryan didn't want his children to experience housing insecurity, so he moved out and let his ex-wife live in their house until she could find a stable situation. He moved in part time with his mom and part time with his friends, but spent some nights in his van. His job performance began to falter, and he was soon let go by his employer. Then, despite all his efforts, he fell behind on paying his bills. It was a domino effect.

Ryan's top priority was to make sure that his children were stable and secure. Through the divorce, he was able to keep the house and shared custody of his children. He was also helping his ex-wife find a place of her own and get new furniture, wanting the transition to be as smooth and easy as possible for their children. Once his ex-wife reached a point where she could sustain herself, Ryan was able to move back into the house. Setting up his ex-wife left him even further behind on payments.

Since our time together in Iraq, we had lost touch with Ryan. He believes that most of the distance was his fault. Eventually, he told us that he didn't want to come forward to explain the shame he felt over his personal and financial circumstances. The severity of his housing issues wasn't realized until after he got remarried. The stresses of having a new wife and two children made him ask, "What are we going to do?" Not much time had passed when he called Dale and said, "Battle Buddy, this is what's going on. I don't know what else to do. I need help."

Although helping someone who was behind on their mortgage payments hadn't been something Purple Heart Homes was accustomed to doing, we couldn't let Ryan down. He was our battle buddy, so we had to figure out a way to help him. Thanks to some of our staff members, we were able to map out a plan to avoid foreclosure on Ryan's home.

A sense of relief entered Ryan's life after we were able to help him with his home. He soon became reemployed at his old job. Once he had a stable home and started working again, things had a little better outlook. Sometimes you fall so far behind, you can't just get caught up on your own. Through Purple Heart Homes, we were able to act as the liaison between Ryan, the bank, and the law firm that was handling the foreclosure to put the brakes on everything until he could get funding and get back on track. A simple hand up and conversation were all that was needed.

Ryan has told us that Purple Heart Homes changed his life. He explained, "We can probably go twenty years without talking to each other, but if one of us needs something, boom, we're there. That is the bond of brothers in arms. Just a simple phone call made it feel as though we were back in Iraq together, having each other's backs."

Now that Ryan is no longer consumed with solving his own financial problems, he is able to think of other veterans. Part of his job as the Employee Resource Manager puts him in charge of structuring resource groups for his employees. He has taken the initiative to organize a veterans' resource guide to better serve that demographic in his company. He keeps asking, "How can we, as a company, support our veterans and be more there for them?"

One project that Ryan finished working on recently was a partnership with an organization called Mission 22, a 501(c)(3) nonprofit that focuses on awareness and assistance for the veteran suicide rate. The organization focuses on three levels. First, they focus on the specific veteran. Whether the veteran needs counseling or medical help, Mission 22 will do what it takes to avoid the potential loss of another veteran. Second, the organization places focus on the family of the veteran. A large number of families don't receive the education they need in order to learn how to live with the veteran. The goal there is to provide the necessary resources that will help the family to better understand what is going on inside of the veteran's head. Third, Mission 22 focuses on the community. Communities have the option to reach out to Mission 22 and help establish veteran aid groups to help the soldiers within their specific community. Ryan shared with us, "We did one project with them that ended up raising a little over $3,800 for Mission 22. My one work site has over 900 employees, and nearly every one of those employees was able to spread awareness in some way, shape, or form."

Mission 22 is something that Ryan is excited about. When veterans get to a place where they feel comfortable enough to start giving back themselves, it's a true sign of successful reintegration, and something we're always happy to see.

Dave Morrell

It was 1965, just outside Fort Lee in the small town of Hopewell, Virginia. All the kids Dave Morrell went to school with were military brats, so he was well acquainted with Army culture. He hated high school, and dropped out during his senior year to join the Army Special Forces.

After getting his GED, Dave went on to serve three tours in Vietnam. He spent some time talking with us, and he shared, "I grew up fast. I was with the unit that later became Delta Force and I had a nice, young lieutenant, Hugh Shelton, who was my boss. Shelton later became the commanding general of the Joint Chiefs of Staff. Even back then, he was very likable and well-respected."

Dave Morrell while on patrol in the jungles of Vietnam

Three years passed before Dave went back home and entered the College of William and Mary, studying business and graduating with honors. He enjoyed school this time. Because he was in a military town, he didn't encounter protesters like many other Vietnam veterans faced across the country. The dean of his college was a retired colonel and the dean of students was a reservist, Marine Major. Many other veterans were students as well. There was a great sense of camaraderie throughout the college.

When Dave graduated from college, he soon got married and

moved to Richmond. He told us, "It was a lousy forty miles away. No job and newly married, I went out on job interviews. One day, I went to this one major company for an interview. The employer looked at me, and he said, 'Well, if we ever decide to hire baby killers, we'll give you a call.' That was my first experience of being put down for being a veteran. It was just so devastating that I came home and locked myself in for two or three days before I could go out again. I was afraid that I was going to run into more of that."

Dave Morrell [center] after receiving military service award while in Vietnam

Dave doesn't know when the symptoms began. He recalled, "I just became what I became. I was changing jobs every three years. I wasn't fired, but just changing jobs because I needed to be around different people. I didn't hate the people I was around, but mostly I just couldn't stand to be around people in general. I went through a couple of marriages. I just became angry and even now I'm not able to be around a lot of people." Dave didn't know that he was suffering from post-traumatic stress. Little did he know that post-traumatic stress wouldn't be the only long-lasting impact he would be confronted with from his time in Vietnam.

The United States sprayed nearly 20 million gallons of Agent Orange in Vietnam, eastern Laos, and parts of Cambodia as part of the aerial defoliation program known as Operation Ranch Hand. Manufactured by Monsanto and Dow Chemical, the compound was used to destroy jungle foliage that gave cover to enemy troops, and to kill the crops of the rural population so they'd be starved out and driven into the American-controlled cities. The spraying reached its peak between 1967 and 1969—the years during which Dave was there.

"It was made to clean the jungle out so that the guys could go on patrol. Of course, back then, we didn't know going in there that the chemical was in the air and it was going to cause all of these problems, health-wise. I've had heart problems and skin cancer. Over the years, I've developed diabetes and couldn't heal. Eleven years ago, I lost my left leg, and I ended up losing my right leg just recently," Dave shares.

While in Vietnam, soldiers were told not to worry about the chemical, that it was harmless. After they returned home, veterans began to suspect that their ill health, their wives' miscarriages, or children—and now grandchildren—born with birth defects, could be caused by the exposure. Some veterans began to file claims in 1977 to Veterans Affairs for disability payments for healthcare, but their claims were denied unless they could prove that the condition began while they were in service, or within one year of their discharge.

In April 1993, Veterans Affairs compensated only 486 victims, although it had received disability claims from 39,419 soldiers who had been exposed to Agent Orange while serving in Vietnam.

Dave Morrell sits on this trike awaiting the start
of a poker run to raise funds for charity.

When Dave was diagnosed with diabetes in 1994, he wasn't told that it was due to his exposure to Agent Orange. He told us, "I didn't find out until about ten years ago... same thing with PTS. I went forty-some years not knowing that I couldn't keep a job for more than three years because I just couldn't stand to be around other people and this was related to Vietnam. I was ignorant of that fact. It wasn't until I moved to North Carolina when I started finding out about all of this stuff that was related to Vietnam."

Dave moved to North Carolina in 2006. He joined the local Veterans of Foreign Wars (VFW) and members there began to help him understand the causes of his physical and emotional issues. They advised him to go talk with Veteran Affairs. "I went to the V.A., and sure enough, they diagnosed me for diabetes and PTS. All of my problems were attributed to Vietnam and the exposure of Agent Orange. I found out later in life what caused my problems. Luckily—or, unluckily—they gave me disability pay. I'd rather be healthy than have the disability pay, but it is what it is," Dave told us.

For all those years, Dave didn't know why he was afraid of being around people, or why he couldn't keep a job or stay in a marriage. He said, "I didn't know they had a name for it, or that it was related to Vietnam. Of course, the V.A. started sending me to a psychiatrist and they began treating me with medication and whatever—and a lot of talking. Come to find out—and friends of mine all agree—the best therapy the V.A. ever gave me was a service dog."

Dave Morrell poses by the American flag just outside of his front door for Reader's Digest after the completion of his home renovation by Purple Heart Homes.

Dave has a service dog almost always with him. The dog came from a local organization called Patriot Rovers, which train the animals and donates them to veterans with PTS. Dave speaks fondly of his dog, telling us, "These dogs are about $10,000 to train and I was given one for free. He senses when I'm having nightmares and wakes me up. When I go out in public, he can tell when I start getting nervous around people. We'll go to Walmart and he'll put himself between other people and me. He'll purposely go up to someone and want that person to pet him or whatever. He's forcing that person to keep their distance from me, that's what he's actually doing."

His dog's name is Ryan. Ryan's name is very special. Gold Star is a term used to refer to a family who has lost a loved one in military service. Gold Star mothers are given the privilege of naming the service dogs for Patriot Rovers after veterans who have lost their lives. It just so happens that Dave's dog is named after Christopher Ryan Barton, who Dave helped bury with the Patriot Riders. The family—the widow and parents—became good friends with Dave, and of course, they were thrilled when he received the dog that was named after their loved one.

Ryan is a Golden Retriever with a little Australian Shepherd in him. Retrievers seem to make some of the best service dogs because of their temperament. "He's six years old. When he's with me, he will not leave my side. It almost gets to the point where I'm tripping over him because he's got to be down there by my feet. I always laugh and say he's better than a wife; I can put him in the garage and he'll still wag his tail when I open that door on him—he's never tried to hit me with a frying pan. Lord knows what's going to happen the day something happens to him. He's my best friend—my best buddy," Dave's face softens as he speaks of his greatest companion.

Richard's Coffee Shop and Military Museum also play a part in Dave's stories. "On Thursdays, it's packed with veterans. Ryan normally goes with me and he's almost become the mascot. All the World War II veterans just want to hug and play with him, which I allow. When he can't come with me, they always ask where he's at. I tell them that they pay too much attention to him and ignore me, so I left him at home," Dave chuckles.

As an amputee, life at home became increasingly difficult for Dave. The doorways were too narrow for him to get through with his walker or wheelchair. He would have to crawl on his hands and knees to get into the bathroom, and hoisting himself into the tub for a shower was difficult and painful.

When Cory Collins, Dave's friend and fellow veteran, was about to lose a leg, we and other volunteers from Purple Heart Homes rehabbed Cory's house to make it livable for him when he came back from the hospital. That's how Dave found out about our organization.

Cory told us Dave's story. We met Dave at the coffee shop in Mooresville, and soon afterward went to his house to assess the situation. We told him that we would build a whole new addition that included an accessible bathroom. Dave became our first major project. Up until that point, we were only rehabbing bathrooms, putting in ramps, and doing different types of small projects for people. Dave's house was our first project with a complete addition—a bedroom with ramps leading out to his back porch, a completely accessible bathroom, and doors that he can get through with his wheelchair.

Purple Heart Homes began construction on Dave's house in January 2011, and it was completed by April of that year. Volunteers worked every day. The number of volunteers depended on the type of specialty work that was required for the day. On the opening day when we broke ground and took out trees with a Bobcat, there were at least fifty people on hand. They were neighbors, friends, veterans of all eras, and Len Bealer, the contractor who agreed to manage the project as a pro bono service for Purple Heart Homes. Four or five electricians came, some from over a hundred miles away, to do the wiring. A handful of plumbers, concrete finishers, electricians, tile companies, and painters all chipped in to donate their services for several days as well.

Besides adding the bathroom and bedroom and widening the doorways, we added ramps wherever necessary. We also tore out the carpets throughout the house and replaced them with hardwood floors, since it's difficult to roll a wheelchair over carpet. Dave told us, "Having that handicap bathroom is great. I have a wonderful shower that I can either wheel my chair straight into or transfer to a seat that's built in."

Framing Day from Kenneth Bealer Homes in background and Ron Fry on left. Ron also served with Dale and John in Iraq.

Five years after the work was completed, and with three major surgeries behind him, Dave became a double amputee. The effects of Agent Orange, diabetes, and constant pain led him to electively have his other leg removed. He shared, "Thank God this work was done, because as a single amputee, I could learn to make do. I don't know what I'd do now if Purple Heart Homes hadn't fixed this house. I have an electric wheelchair and I run around that downstairs like it's a racecourse, thanks to the way it was fixed for me. The last thing that I'm worried about is ending up in a nursing home. I want to take care of myself for as long as possible. Not that I refuse help... but pride keeps us from realizing that there are just certain times when all of us need help."

*Crew of volunteers from Blythe Construction out of Charlotte, NC,
pour concrete for Dave Morrell's rear patio and exit ramps.*

Thinking back on the four months of construction, Dave said, "It was like a dream. Each day I'd wake up and wonder, 'Is this going to end?' However, the volunteers kept showing up and the next thing you know, I had this beautiful home. It's really changed my life." About those who helped on the project, he said, "I met a lot of new friends who I could stand to be around. You two guys are more like brothers than anything else. You guys are angels of mercy. What you guys do is wonderful. I really think the world of Purple Heart Homes and I wish that I could do more for them. With my health, the best thing I can do is spread the word about what a good organization it is."

There's a story in *Reader's Digest* that has a photograph of Dave positioned in between the two of us. He's the short guy in the middle. That photograph was taken before Dave became a double amputee. Now, his perspective has changed. Dave told us, "I might be sixty-nine years old, but I'm still growing. I always wanted to be tall—I'm tired of being short. Of course, having two prosthetics, they can make me any height that I want. I went from being five-foot-eight to six feet tall thanks to my new legs. I tell everybody now, 'What's four inches taller, but really two feet shorter?' It's me!"

John, Dave, and Dale pose for a photo to be used for Reader's Digest in 2011 sharing Dave and Purple Heart Homes' story.

Dave credits Purple Heart Homes with changing his life for the better, and for actually saving the lives of other veterans. He expressed with joy, "The great part about this organization is that they help service people from all wars, not just from the most recent wars." He added with a change in his expression, "There's a lot of great organizations out there, but unfortunately for other age groups and myself, most of those organizations only want to help the younger veterans from Iraq and Afghanistan. There are a ton of assistance programs out there that could be an unbelievable benefit to many veterans, but I can't get them because my service was forty years ago during Vietnam. The Iraq and Afghanistan veterans should get everything they can. They deserve it, they really do. It has nothing to do with them, but it's a stark reminder of my job interview in 1972. Are we still not worth it?"

Completed addition on back of Dave Morrell's home,
providing him with a fully accessible first floor living space

Dave continues on his point, "There are still a few World War II veterans around, quite a few Korean veterans, and definitely a lot of Vietnam veterans, but we're pretty much placed on the backburner. There are some organizations out there that help all of us, but Purple Heart Homes was the first one I ever encountered. Purple Heart Homes has taken on the task of helping everybody that they can, while other organizations have limited their services. It's a shame. Of course, it runs to economics too. How much can you afford to do for people? How many people can you help?"

There are more wounded Vietnam veterans still living than all other veterans from all previous wars combined. Dave says, "We have the highest number of wounded veterans that are still on this planet—which is a good thing. Unfortunately, one death is one death too many when it comes to war. People don't realize that the soldier is the guy who wants war the least. Nobody wants to go to war. They do it for our country and it's a necessary thing. However, if we're given the choice between having war and peace, we'd all choose peace."

Scott Emory

Scott Emory was born in Gastonia, North Carolina. When he was eleven years old, his family moved to Statesville, about an hour's drive to the north. The military is a strong part of Scott's heritage. Most of all the men on his father's side of the family had been in the service. He explained to us, "We've had family members who served as militia before the National Guard, reservists and active duty throughout all of our generations." On his mother's side of the family, most of them joined the National Guard. Every generation of his family has served in every major war or conflict: his great-grandfather in World War I, his grandfather and great-uncles in World War II and Korea, and his father was on a K-9 team in Okinawa during the Vietnam era.

After graduating from high school in 1988, Scott joined the Marine Corps, planning to make a career of it for at least the next twenty years. His nineteenth birthday passed while he was in boot camp. Scott recalled, "They sort of razzed me about being the oldest in the platoon, calling me 'the old man' and whatnot." He enjoyed boot camp. He expected and wanted the training to be difficult, as he knew that the drill instructors were preparing him for the hostile situations he would encounter in combat. He continued, "Before I went to boot camp, I was told by other Marines that if you stay in the Marine Corps for twenty years, expect to be in combat at least once. To have the mindset, that even though you're serving during peacetime, train as if you could get injured or killed, and expect the worst."

Scott went to Infantry Training School after boot camp, and three months later, he received his orders for his first unit assignment. Soon after arrival, the unit was getting ready for hostilities in Panama. Scott reflected with nostalgia, "You can imagine a guy that's only been in service for a few months getting ready to go into combat. I kept thinking that I knew enough to get myself into trouble." Most of the attached units were sent to Panama, but as his unit was about to board the transport to leave, the mission was cancelled.

Scott, out on a training mission just prior to deploying for Desert Storm

The disappointment of not being able to go on that mission stuck with Scott for a long time. He was eager to put all of his training to work. Eventually, he was sent to Okinawa in 1990, when the United States returned bases in the Philippines to the Filipino Marines and Army. Six months later, he came back and went straight into desert training at Twentynine Palms, not knowing what he was training for. A few months later, in December, his feet were on the ground over in Saudi Arabia. "For all intents and purposes, it looked just like Twentynine Palms."

At that point, Scott's unit was a couple of hundred miles south of the front, which was nowhere close to where the unit needed to be.

As they all made their way north, Scott was injured—accidentally severing a nerve in his foot. He was hospitalized in a Marine hospital for two weeks. While he was recuperating, Christmas came—as did his twenty-first birthday.

Once those two weeks passed, Scott was able to get back to work. He shared with us, "We were setting up for our push north. January 17 is the day that the actual bombings—the air war—started. When I would get time off from guard duty, I would look up in the sky. I could lay on the back of a five-ton, look up, and see all these B-52 bombers going over. It was like the stars were moving and were completely out of alignment. That's how many bombers were going over at one time."

Scott's mission was in a logistics train. Coalition forces were expecting an increase in chemical attacks from missiles and chemical mines that had been placed in the area years before. He told us, "They were trying to find an NBC team—a chemical decontamination team—and my name came up. They asked me if I wanted to be part of it, and, being the smart Marine that nobody thinks I am, I told myself that was pretty much the safest place I could be. I didn't mind being on the frontlines."

Scott driving a HUMVEE while saying 'hi' to folks back home

The team would come in behind a unit and set up a chemical decontamination site at every stop, which was dangerous because they were forced to set up tents with mechanics sitting in one spot for an extended amount of time, making them an easy target.

One of the chemicals that Saddam's army used was a blister agent, something similar to mustard gas. Scott explained to us, "Whenever the rounds would hit, we'd see the white puffs of smoke. When the units would get hit, they would come back to us for decontamination. The chemical suits would be cut off, and the gas masks and personnel would be decontaminated. It was the only shower these guys had in a month. If some of the casualties came in on stretchers, we'd have to do the same thing to them, if they were unable to move under their own power. Then they'd be transferred to another stretcher. Decontaminating vehicles was pretty much the same procedure."

The chemical rounds were only one part of the contamination that troops would receive. Perhaps, the worst were the oil fires. In an attempt to disrupt coalition aircraft and slow the advance of our troops, Iraqi combat engineers dug trenches, filled them with oil, and ignited them, sending smoke plumes high into the sky. They also spilled oil in the Persian Gulf to keep US Marines from making an amphibious landing. It's estimated that they spilled as much as eleven million barrels, several times the size of the Exxon Valdez spill. This type of scorched earth tactic eventually led to the destruction of 85 percent of Kuwait's oil wells.

"I knew that as soon as I stopped at the next area to set up, I could decontaminate myself if I needed to. I worried more about the stuff overhead of us. When Saddam lit up the oil, we got covered with the fallout of the oil fires. We were in smoke for the entire time. I mean, it was a constant thing. You couldn't get that smoke out of your nostrils. I worried about that more than I did the chemicals at the time," Scott recalled, as his expression turned heavy.

"I shouldn't be sitting here. There must be a higher calling for me," Scott was referring to that particular February night in 1991, when his unit began taking on mortar fire. He continued, "At 4:00 a.m., we were coming over the ridge and the scene was something else to see: three thousand vehicles inside of two thousand meters—two grid squares about a mile and a half long. It was unreal. We were stacked on top of each other. When the Saudis and Iraqis saw that, they started throwing mortar and artillery fire down range. Our unit began taking some major mortar fire, and a piece of the mortar flew up and went underneath my helmet. I was pretty lucky... I woke up with four or five guys standing over me. They asked me if I was alright, and I said, 'Yeah, I'm fine. Just get the hell out of here. I don't want to get hit twice.'" Scott was unaware that he had suffered a traumatic brain injury at that point.

The war started on January 17, 1991, and ended quickly after just five weeks. A ground assault that began on February 24 led to a decisive victory for the coalition forces as they liberated Kuwait and advanced into Iraqi territory. They declared a ceasefire just one hundred hours after the ground campaign started.

Scott expressed, "Believe it or not, I was only there for four months. Once the hostilities stopped, we stayed to guard the road going into Kuwait for about two weeks. We were able to decompress for a little bit, but still had our guard duty and that kind of stuff. By that time, the logistics train started collecting what the unit hadn't used—such as the grenades and rounds. The chemical decontamination unit was packing everything back onto trucks. They sent us back down south so that we could consolidate and recover a bit more as we left the hostile areas. Our unit got situated down south and then we got on the planes to go home.

In 1995, Scott switched his military occupational specialty (MOS) from the infantry to artillery. He worked as a mechanic on the M198 Howitzer, an eight-ton device towed behind a vehicle that shoots 155 mm high explosives and chemical rounds—even nuclear rounds. One day in early 1997, Scott and a fellow Marine were moving a gun around by hand, while a third Marine was in charge of safety procedures. During a point of distraction, the gun pivoted on its two wheels, with Scott ending up underneath it. He recalled, "I'm a strong, six-foot-three guy, but even with my strength, I was no match for eight tons of metal hanging over me. The third Marine was injured while he was trying to keep me from being crushed by the gun. Regardless of his attempt, the gun won."

The weight fell on Scott's lower back and compressed two vertebrae. He shared, "I was lucky that day. However, what the doctors didn't know at the time—even though they did x-rays, MRIs, and CT scans—was that the injury created a pinhole in one of my disks. I didn't know for about six years that the disk had been leaking fluid into my spinal canal all that time. A doctor at the V.A. said that I was pretty lucky, because that situation could have paralyzed me and put me in a wheelchair."

Scott met Rachelle in December 1996, just before he was injured in the Howitzer accident. He knew right away that he wanted to marry her. Even after she learned the extent of his injuries, she stuck by him, and he knew she was the one. He told us, "I asked her to marry me while I was going through treatment and deploying at the same time. Within nine months of Rachelle and I meeting and getting married, I deployed twice, each time for three months. Rachelle knew what she was getting into, being a Marine's wife from the start. As rough as it has been on her, she's been there ever since. There have been rough patches just like any other couple, but we're still together all these years later." He continued, "To be honest, I was pretty lucky because I had already gotten injured before I asked her to marry me. She still married me, even after the doctors told us that I might end up getting out of the Marine Corps due to my injuries. I was very fortunate in the fact that she was one of the few spouses that was made to be a Marine Corps spouse. I saw so many Marines getting discharged due to injuries, and then their marriage ends up in a divorce." Divorce is a fact of life in the military. While the civilian divorce rate remained consistent into the 1990s, the Marine Corps saw its overall divorce rate increase to 77 percent between 1980 and 1993.

Scott sits and rests with his service dog, Chance, after a walk with his family.

After the Howitzer accident, Scott spent the next two years trying to get back to normal, but his plan for a twenty-plus year career in the military came to an end in 1999 after the Marines medically discharged him. He explained to us, "The Marine Corps gave me a lump sum for the eleven years that I was in and basically said, 'See you later.' Eleven years in, and then I was out of a job. I don't hold any bad feelings toward them, because it is what it is; it's a business."

The mortar fragment that slipped underneath Scott's helmet still sits inside of his home, to serve as a reminder of the hope and resilience within himself, and all of the struggles that he's gone through to get to where he is today.

Scott used the lump sum that he received from the Marines to buy a small mobile home in the country for Rachelle and himself. They needed to add a well and septic system, and after those additions, the money that they were given was gone. Scott remembers, "For that first year, we were flat out broke, but we had a roof over our heads. I looked at my worried wife and said, 'Look, they can take the electricity, but they can't take our home.' Our well was gravity-fed, so we were going to keep having water. We weren't paying for septic, so they could take everything else and all we had to worry about was food."

Within that year, things started to look up for a little bit. "I finally got my rating from the V.A., and I started going to a lot of appointments, which kept me—at that time—from trying to get a job. Nobody would even touch me because I was going to the V.A. four to five times a week for my back. It was there that I discovered why I had been experiencing various types of issues all throughout the left side of my body." Scott tried to help others when he could. "I would be at the V.A. and see some of the younger guys who had just gotten back from Iraq discouraged because they couldn't get help. I would guide them to the Patient Advocates that I knew and get them pointed in the right direction as much as I could, even though my own situation wasn't the best."

The couple continued to struggle throughout the next ten years. Rachelle worked as a radiographer to pay the bills. Scott used the G.I. Bill to go back to college and studied computer technology in Winston-Salem, North Carolina. He kept looking for work, but the jobs never came through. "Every interview I went to, the employers always brought up something negative. I had one employer tell me that I was a liability because of my back issue," Scott lamented.

After their two sons were born, Scott became a stay-at-home dad, taking care of the boys while Rachelle worked full-time. In 2009, they had outgrown the mobile home and bought a small house in the country—a foreclosure that needed work. One day, Scott was working in the crawl space underneath the house when his back gave out. He re-lived that moment when he explained to us, "Nobody was home. I hit a pipe, and then I couldn't move. I couldn't even turn over to crawl on my back. This was in the middle of the day, so I ended up laying there for a few hours, trying to get out by myself. I heard one of my neighbors pull into his driveway, so I yelled. He heard me and grabbed another guy to come under my house. They pulled me out by my boots."

Scott was already familiar with Purple Heart Homes. He met John a couple of years earlier, at a church event honoring the local heroes, and John walked up to shake his hand. Later, while looking at the Purple Heart Homes website, Scott discovered that they had done a project for a Marine that he served with, someone he had been trying to reconnect with for over twenty years. Scott revealed, "I went on the website to sign up as a volunteer to help the guy. I found out, he had been looking for me just as long as I had been looking for him." Scott had been thinking about some home improvements for himself, and thought he'd drop by Purple Heart Homes to ask if he could use their general contractor. He had a little money saved, and figured that he could do the work piecemeal. On that day, Scott reintroduced himself to John and met Dale for the first time, intending to volunteer to help his friend.

Instead, Scott recalled us saying, "We really don't make referrals, why don't you put in an application?" Scott hemmed and hawed a bit because he didn't really want the help. He wanted to do it himself. He admitted, "That was the only thing to keep me feeling like I'm still a man. You want to do it yourself. You don't want anyone to help. The military teaches you how to adapt and overcome, not to ask for help. It's hard, but I believe that being a Veteran and working with an organization founded by veterans helps make it acceptable and more comfortable for me. Sometimes, that requires hearing what you don't want to hear. The job requires tough love at times."

He had to admit though; he needed a bathtub big enough for him to fit into. He confessed, "There were times when I was in so much pain that I was crawling through the house. The bathroom was so small that I had to use the sink, countertop, and tub just to move around. Like I said, I'm six-foot-three. When I would crawl in for a bath, I needed to kick my leg over the tub full of water, then fold my legs back under me just to sit down and soak. I would soak in the hottest water possible, just so I could stretch out to make the pain go away in order for me to get up and walk for a little bit."

After submitting his application to Purple Heart Homes, several weeks went by and he hadn't heard anything. Scott thought that we weren't going to help him, until our vetting committee called him and said, "We've got some news. You got approved. We're going to do what needs to be done." Then, we took a project manager and contractor over to evaluate Scott's home. Just a few weeks later, we were headed back with an architectural plan and renderings. The plan was to enlarge the bathroom by tearing the wall out between the bath and utility room. The rendering showed an addition behind the house, with a laundry room, mudroom, and an exercise room for Scott. After seeing what the rendition entailed, Scott told us, "The biggest thing for me, other than the tub, was that I couldn't do any type of physical fitness at all. When I was in the military, and even before, I was a fitness freak. When that aspect of my life was taken away, I kept gaining weight, which caused more pain. I called my wife while the project manager was at the house and told her what all they were planning on doing. She started crying. They were definitely happy tears, because these guys were basically giving us the home that everybody deserves. We felt like somebody finally cared about us."

Another addition that Purple Heart Homes planned for Scott's house was a front porch. Scott admitted, "There were really two reasons behind the request. One, I told John about my childhood, how everyone in my family had front porches. I've always felt that having one makes visitors feel more welcome at your home. When someone knocks on the front door and there's just a little concrete stoop outside, they're going to get rained on. The other reason: my kids like to play in the front yard. I always had to look outside of the front window to see them, or I would sit on our concrete stoop for five minutes and need to get up because I felt numb from the waist down. Those were the two biggest reasons why I wanted a front porch, being able to sit outside, watch my kids play, see my neighbors, and watch people walking by." Scott had a strong desire to be connected to his community.

After the flurry of construction activity and the excitement of having the entire community volunteering on the site was over, Scott's family adjusted to their expanded home. Scott now had a place to regain his passion for keeping physically fit. He shared with gratitude, "Purple Heart Homes did that extra room to give me a space to just go, be myself, and exercise. Right now, I'm a hand cyclist. I've got a hand cycle on a bike trainer back there. I go back there during inclement weather, when I'm unable to go outside, and work out on my bike. Now, I can keep my body physically fit, for the most part. That helps out quite a bit. It helps your mindset, too. I didn't want to go outside before Purple Heart Homes came in and worked on our house."

Not only did the new room give Scott a place to exercise, but it also gave him a place to be alone and feel safe whenever his nightmares from Desert Storm would keep him awake. Now, the rest of his family can sleep through the night.

Scott is grateful for all of the ways Purple Heart Homes changed his family's life. Before, the family picked up the slack for the things Scott couldn't do. He shared, "At that time, even my three-year-old was picking up things for me whenever I couldn't get a hold of them. I would drop my keys and my son would come running across the room to pick them up for me. I would grunt, wiggle, and fall down on the floor in order to get my keys before he could get there, because it got to the point where I couldn't stand it anymore. To me, it was taking their childhood away. Being dependent on them all of the time made me feel less of a man than I already felt, especially when a three-year-old says, 'Daddy, let me pick that up for you.' My wife

153

always had to do stuff, too. She's helpful and everything, but even the best people in the world need a break, much less the best spouses. I always wanted her to find a girlfriend to go shopping or have a party with, but she wouldn't do that because she was worried that something might happen to me. The kids wouldn't go down the road to play with other kids because they wanted to be present for me. I got tired of that; I didn't want to be a burden or excuse. That's the biggest thing that I think Purple Heart Homes has given us: a little bit more of our individuality as a family. It's made us stronger as a family."

When Scott was deployed, he would jot down ideas or impressions and later write poems about his experiences. He told us, "I actually started just after high school. My favorite poet was always Robert Frost, because he didn't really rhyme things, he just told a story. That's more of my thing. Most of my stuff took three or four months to write. I'm featured in a book that a lady put together of poems by Marines in combat, poems from different eras of war. I'm the type that when I write a poem, I quit reading it because it's always too emotional for me. Once my poems are put in the books, I can read them, but I often skim through them because there are certain aspects that everybody is going to go through after combat. You're going to think about it. You can't just forget about it and throw it off to the side. I can't do that."

I DIED THERE

By: Fmr. Sgt. C.S. Emory
USMC/ 2/2 ed MarDiv.
Persian Gulf, 1990-1991

As my thoughts wander,
to things that could happen.
My heart races,
adrenaline flows like blood.
We stand at the ready,
for the things that are to happen.

A last-minute gear check,
we each shake hands and say,
"See you when the storm's over".
Turning away walking back,
I think of what might be
Looking back only once,
I see a dense cloud over my friend…
…my brother.
That strange smoke overwhelms the evening,
on things that are to be.
Like a blanket,
darkness it comes.
Morning the command,
silently passed throughout.
We have landed,
As Marines before us,
knowing that death will be found there.
The music of artillery precedes,
as we move forward.
"Shake and bake 'em boys,
steel on target.
As we meet our enemies,
one thought precedes the fight.
Get home in one piece,
our minds function as one, as
rounds ring out.
Incoming! shouted,
we take a hit.
Ticked-off and now scared,
anger and fear combine.
My enemies *will* precede me,
if I am to die today.
As I protect my friend…
…my Nation.
We fix 'em and feed 'em,

our prisoners,
While they kill our brothers.
A young boy comes into sight, enemy,
his face is beaten.
And yet, he sits on the stretcher,
motionless, a blackness in his eyes.
This is our enemy, his mind and heart
broken in the fight…
…what Respect he has earned.
One hundred hours in, the storm's
over…
…but my brother doesn't smile.
I returned home to,
find a war in my mind always,
A piece of me gone…
…dead inside.

Lauren Hogan

Lauren Hogan was born and spent her first seven years in Vermont, living there until her family moved to the Seattle suburb of Bothell, Washington. She doesn't have many memories of Vermont, except for a yard full of decorations, the fields where she played with her two older sisters, and Ben and Jerry's ice cream.

Lauren wasn't enthusiastic about the high school she attended in Bothell, so she switched to an alternative school while she was in the tenth grade. She felt as though she wasn't learning anything, so she dropped out and got her GED when she was sixteen years old.

Lauren Hogan's high school graduation photo

Feeling uninspired after taking a couple of online college classes, Lauren decided to enlist in the Army after she turned eighteen. She explained her reasoning to us, "My older sister's best friend signed up for the Army. I thought that if she could do it, I could do it, too. Then, I could go straight into a career and not have to worry about wasting my parents' money on college."

Lauren Hogan

What compels a young woman to join the Army? A study done by the Pew Foundation found that just like men, 80 percent of female veterans say they joined to serve our country or to receive educational benefits. Almost three-quarters of them say that they wanted to see more of the world, and about just as many joined to gain job skills. One key difference in the reasons why men and women joined the military is that nearly twice as many females say they joined because jobs were hard to find.

Lauren in the orderly room of her first permanent duty station

Lauren wishes that she could have been given a little more career guidance in the beginning. She told us, "I did well on my exams and they told me that I could basically do whatever I wanted, but they didn't tell me anything about the military culture. I told them that I wanted to be a mechanic. My dad had been teaching me since I was sixteen years old. My mom bought junky cars and my dad was always fixing them. I would help him often, so I knew that I was good at that." When the recruiters learned that Lauren wanted to be a mechanic, they told her that there would be an opening for her at Fort Lewis, Washington, after she returned from basic training.

Lauren poses with teammates in motor pool.

Although basic training was a challenge for Lauren, she claims that she had fun during that time. "You learn how to have fun in the situations you find yourself in during basic training." Her advanced individual training (AIT) took place at Aberdeen Proving Grounds in Maryland, lasted for thirteen weeks, and she returned to Washington afterwards. She shared with us, "I was told on my first day that I was going to be in Iraq in less than a week. I felt like it wasn't fair, because I had two guys from my AIT go to Fort Lewis, and then there was another guy—we don't even know what happened to him. I don't know if he went AWOL[9], or what. Another guy got to go to Qatar; he got to travel to, what we consider to be, a vacation spot, and get paid the same amount as me."

Before Lauren knew it, she was in Kuwait. She felt like she hadn't been trained properly for the situations she was about to face. She

---

9 An acronym standing for Absent With Out Leave; absent from one's post but without intent to desert.

told us, "I just felt really unprepared. From the time that people in a unit know where they're going, they start training. Then they go to Yakima, or somewhere, and do training exercises there in case something happens. You're just better trained for more specific incidences. I didn't get any of that. They put me in a green flak vest that was too big for me because they didn't have the right materials for women, and then I got an old helmet. Everybody else had newer equipment because they got first dibs."

Soon, Lauren was in Iraq, at Forward Operating Base Marez—a super FOB—just outside of Mosul. It was a beehive of activity, housing several battalions of the 25th Infantry Division from Fort Lewis, the 276th Engineering Battalion from Richmond, Virginia, a unit of the Maine Army National Guard, and numerous private contractors from the Halliburton subsidiary, Kellogg, Brown, and Root. The camp also served as a training facility for the Iraqi National Guard. Nearby Mosul was a mess due to its police stations being occupied by insurgents.

Lauren discovered that she was the low-ranking soldier in her area. Everybody expected her to do everything for them. It was a very strict environment. She was assigned to work as a light-wheeled vehicle mechanic, and in the first few days, received training from the people that her unit had been sent to replace. She recalled, "I remember that they stuffed all of the females into one building. We had to be in a room with twenty other females. I was the lowest E1 Private that you could be, and I was in a room with E6 Staff Sergeants who had been there for six or more years. I wasn't really used to the ranking system. I was used to privates and drill Sergeants— the low people and the people who told you what to do. I wasn't used to *everybody* telling me what to do."

She spent the first couple of weeks getting acclimated to the place. It was uncomfortable for Lauren as a woman on the base. She shared, "The men called us Desert Queens right off the bat, no matter how you acted. They said that they could smell you coming by your shampoo, or soap, or whatever. I cut my hair short, but I should've just shaved my head, because it's obvious that if your hair is longer than shaved, you're not a male."

Females were prohibited from going off of the base, unable to go along on supply convoys, or other missions. They were told that the enemy had offered a $100,000 bounty on women's heads. "That's what they told us, at least. I stayed on the base the entire time and was as comfortable as you could be in a place like that," Lauren said.

There were only three other females in Lauren's platoon who were mechanics; most of the others were nurses. That made her feel lonely and isolated, so she hung out with the guys in the service and recovery group. She told us, "Since I was in service and recovery, they took me under their wing and treated me better than most of the other guys. I would spend my time off with them, playing video games. They were the only people who I connected with genuinely."

Then, there was the guard duty. They were on constant rotation, four hours on and four hours off, in twenty-four-hour segments. Lauren reflected, "You got paired with any random person that was in our whole company. There were nurses and generator mechanics—all different types of jobs—and we would get paired randomly with a different person, sometimes the same person, on guard duty. You would meet someone new pretty much every time you went on duty. Then, you might never see them again." Lauren settled into a grinding routine at Marez: sad, alone, and on edge because of the constant barrage of incoming mortars that hit the base sporadically. Little did she realize, things were about to get worse.

One of the favorite places for anyone stationed at Marez was the mess hall. In the new world of privatized wars, mess halls were no longer run by grizzled Army cooks dishing out crummy grub. Now, they were slick operations overseen by Halliburton, and little expense was spared. Like many dining facilities, it was a soft-sided tent. The word "tent" conjures up an image of a small and confining space, but the mess hall at Marez was nothing like that. From the outside, it appeared as large as an airplane hangar, with a soaring, peaked roof. Inside were long, orderly rows of tables and chairs, enough to accommodate several hundred soldiers, with the ceiling far above. Banks of powerful spotlights hung down, illuminating the entire place day and night.

Everyone looked forward to mealtimes because the camaraderie provided a break from the chaos outside. Besides, the food was really good. The cooks took special pride in their desserts—especially the cheesecake. The mess hall existed as a place of solace for Lauren. She shared, "The chow hall was the best part of it there. You could get an omelet for breakfast, fries for lunch, and dessert any time you wanted. It was a happy place for the bad deployment."

Meals in the mess hall were one of the few times that the troops would congregate in large groups. Usually, they'd remove their helmets and flak jackets, and rest their weapons on the floor while they ate. On December 21, 2004, there were twinkling lights and tinsel garland strung along the walls, as well as Christmas trees in the corners. This close to the holiday, everybody was missing their families more than ever.

Lauren will remember this day for the rest of her life. She recalled anxiously, "I was working in the motor pool that day. A couple of guys were ready to go to lunch, but I had to lock up my tools first and bring them back to the motor pool. One thing that sticks in my mind is that if I had done that faster, maybe I would have been out of there in time. I was almost done eating when it happened."

All of a sudden, a bomb went off, blowing a huge hole in the roof. Soldiers were thrown out of their chairs and fell amidst a jumble of bloodied lunch trays, overturned tables, shrapnel, and body parts. The tent was filled with rancid smoke, and daylight streamed in through the torn canvas in the roof. Everyone grabbed their weapons and dove for cover. Lauren recalled the horror, "It was behind me. It pushed me forward in my chair and when I looked around—I don't know if I blacked out or what—but it seemed as though everybody was on the floor already. Not like they had been blown out of their chairs, but instead they were ducking and covering because they thought it was a rocket or mortar. Everybody was on the ground, so I got on the ground. I looked at my friend on my left side and he told me that he couldn't feel his legs. I didn't know what to do. He was an E5, and the two guys in front of me were E6s. They had all been serving for ten or more years, or even ready to retire. They knew what to do. They said to just get outside."

Lauren fled to the concrete bunkers outside of the tent and remembered seeing a civilian with blood squirting out of his leg. "I couldn't sit there and watch all of these bloody people. They thought that more incoming rounds were going to be coming in, so we were just waiting there, trying not to get hurt more. I couldn't wait there," Lauren said. She continued, "There were a lot of people running into the tent to help. I went back inside, and in training, they tell you to keep track of your weapons. I asked the guy who said that he couldn't feel his legs if I could take his weapon. I figured it would just get in the way if someone tried to get him out of there. He said, 'Yes,' so I grabbed his weapon and walked back to the motor pool."

At first, everybody thought that they had been hit by a rocket or mortar round. That was the story for days as officials downplayed the idea that it had been the work of a suicide bomber. In reality, it was the work of a suicide bomber—an Iraqi employee who had inside knowledge of the layout and had access to it. He knew when he'd have the greatest impact.

The bomber had entered the mess tent and after approaching a large group of soldiers detonated himself, killing twenty-two people: fourteen US soldiers, four US citizen Halliburton employees, and four Iraqi soldiers allied with the US military. It was the single deadliest suicide attack on American soldiers.

When Lauren got back to the motor pool, she sought out the small office of a guy she knew in the service and recovery group, so she could be away from people and not have to tell everybody there what just happened. She remembered telling the guy there, "I felt a little bit of burning in my back." She asked him if he could look at it. He told her that there was a little piece of shrapnel in her back and that she should go to the medic to have someone there check it out.

She was not quite sure how she got to the medic, but when she got there, it was packed with injured troops. She waited, and they got to her eventually. "They looked at my back and noted what happened, so that I would get the Purple Heart for it. They scrubbed my back with a wire brush, trying to get it out, because it was such a small piece, but it didn't come out. It still shows up on x-rays," Lauren shared.

Lauren receiving deployment awards at a unit ceremony

Soon, Lauren was back on duty in the motor pool. She recalled with remorse, "Nobody wanted to talk about it. Everybody wanted me to suck it up and drive on. I was pretty emotional, because the guy who was sitting next to me had a ball bearing go through his back, about an inch above his belly button. It blew out his stomach. He was in the hospital for three months, and I didn't feel like anybody was even trying to look for him. Nobody heard from him; they just wanted to pretend like it didn't happen,"

It was a difficult time for Lauren. She tried to hide out as often as possible. When she wasn't on duty, she would sleep. Some of the guys gave her a hard time for not wanting to go to the chow hall or internet café. This made Lauren mad, and her anger continued to increase to the point where she started lashing out at her co-workers. Then she felt depressed, which is when the headaches began.

Lauren was always angry, and the headaches wouldn't go away

for three months. She had CAT scans done, but nobody could figure out the cause of her headaches. Veterans Affairs put her on antidepressants. Eventually, they were giving her different types of medicine. After a few tries, her headaches subsided. Lauren settled into a routine again, grinding out the time until she could leave.

Then, her time in Iraq came to an end. She told us, "We went to Kuwait on the way back. Kuwait is a little better than Iraq. It's more of a transition back into civilian life, except that you're sleeping in a tent on cots. Although, you get to eat Burger King and Subway, spend money, buy gifts, and stuff like that."

On the way home, Lauren's plane stopped in Ireland to refuel. Then, it continued on to Washington state. She doesn't remember if anyone from her family was there to greet her when she returned home. Most of Lauren's friends were people she met while in Iraq, and most of them were married men. Her relationship with them changed after they returned to Fort Lewis. That would be alienating enough for her, but on top of that, there wasn't much for anyone to do in the town she lived in. She said to us, "Everybody would go to work, sit around, get off from work, and then they'd drink a lot. That's all anybody did."

Lauren stands for a photo just after her graduation from Basic Training.

Fearing that she was going to get redeployed to Iraq, Lauren decided to leave the Army. Shortly afterwards, she got married and started a family. She got a job as a cashier at a junkyard, where she did well enough to get promoted into buying cars. At that point, Lauren felt like she was back in the military—another male-dominated world where everyone picked on her. She started feeling angry again.

Lauren went back to Veteran Affairs, where they placed her into counseling and prescribed heavy doses of antidepressants. She quit her job at the junkyard and tried selling books on eBay, but that wasn't enough to pay the bills.

While Lauren was in Iraq, she thought mostly about how her life was going to end, and hadn't given much thought to the idea of starting a family. That lack of planning played out in her new marriage. She confessed, "I kind of rushed into it. It didn't really work out. The Army took my husband at the time to Germany, and I didn't go with him. I stayed with my family, so that I didn't have to take care of the baby by myself in another country. Then, we got divorced when our daughter was three years old. I went and hid out from the rest of the world." Lauren moved around the country over the next few years—from Washington to Mississippi, Mississippi to Kentucky, and then Kentucky back to Washington. She remarried and had another child. She told us, "Things kind of went downhill after that."

The couple moved into an RV to save money. But the RV began to fall apart shortly after they acquired it. "Our heater broke and the roof was leaking. Everything else started to fall apart, too," Lauren said. Everything else included her marriage. Her second husband left her among the rest of the chaos. Living as single mother with two young children in an RV with a leaky roof and no heat was the lowest point in Lauren's life.

Catholic Charities stepped in and Lauren was accepted into a program in California for training to become a systems administrator. She told us about her reality after completing the program, saying, "They were supposed to find us jobs. They acted like they had connections with companies and that they were going to do job placement for us. In actuality, they only got us interviews and weren't really connected with any companies. Nothing was guaranteed. It wasn't like the military, where they just sent you away to work."

Most of her fellow students found work, but Lauren had no such luck. She worked with some colleagues on a startup for a few months, but that soon failed. Then, she became a driver for Lyft. Unable to make enough income to get by, letting go of her pride, Lauren finally decided to file for disability with Veterans Affairs.

Remarkably, in a system where people wait as long as three years to get an answer, Lauren received a decision in one month. They determined that she was unemployable, and awarded her a full-income stipend. This gave Lauren some flexibility. She set her sights on North Carolina, where her father had moved to and opened a used furniture store. She told us, "My dad moved back to North Carolina because he grew up in Bessemer City. I asked him if I could live above his store. I still had that mentality of, 'don't work your life away to give somebody else money.'"

Lauren advertised her RV on Craigslist, and it sold quickly. She pocketed the money and moved to North Carolina with her two daughters. They lived in a cluttered space above her father's store on the edge of downtown Bessemer City. It didn't have a shower, and they only had a hotplate for cooking, but at least it was a safe haven. Lauren shared, "It was a furniture store. We had to go to my aunt's house to take a shower. My girls would be trying to do their homework while the store was open... that didn't work out very well." When one of her daughters suffered harassment from other kids on the school bus because she lived above a store and not in a house, Lauren knew they had to find a different place to live.

Although she was helping out at her father's store, Lauren had been wanting to do something more meaningful. She had a need to give back, even when she had so little for herself. Searching for a way she could volunteer to help other veterans, she Googled, "Purple Heart North Carolina." Of course, Purple Heart Homes came up. She said, "I went to the website and saw what they offered, so I signed up to be a volunteer. Although there were not any projects in my area I did maintain contact and followed the organizations activities on Facebook."

There was a rundown house just across the street from her dad's store that had caught her eye. It was a cute, two-bedroom mill house with a front porch. She also noticed that the house had many problems. Despite those problems, she viewed it as an opportunity to get out of living above the store.

The city had been hounding the owner of the house about its derelict condition. The owner was eager to get rid of it, and agreed to sell it to Lauren for $5,000. She still had the cash from selling the RV, so the deal concluded quickly. After she closed on the house, reality set in. She confessed, "It was basically a condemned house when I bought it."

She started working on some repairs, but realized before long that it was too much for her to tackle on her own. Lauren placed an ad on Craigslist and found a former Marine who recently began a contracting business. He said that he could help. Rather than the ticket to freedom she expected it to be, the house soon became more of a millstone around her neck. The city still wanted the house to be torn down, and the "contractors" that she placed her hope in had abandoned the project. Lauren needed to gain approval for an opportunity permit so they could move in, but the scope of work proved to be too much for her limited skills and budget. Things were reaching an impasse, and Lauren felt an all-too-familiar sense of despair.

A friend told her that he knew someone at Purple Heart Homes. Maybe they could help. So, she decided to go online and fill out the application.

A few weeks later, Lauren received a call from Purple Heart Homes. She told us, "At that point, I had listed the house for sale on Craigslist because I was just so sick of trying to do everything by myself. Purple Heart Homes really took us in and gave us hope again." Shortly after the approval, planning began for the renovation. The layout would be reconfigured so that the bathroom could be accessed without having to go through Lauren's bedroom. The old sheetrock would be removed and replaced. There would be new kitchen cabinets and appliances, including a washer and dryer. We also add a convenient entry closet just inside of the front door for coats and boots.

On the first day, the crew of volunteers showed up to begin work. Lauren was there, along with a television crew videotaping the project for a T.V. segment featuring Purple Heart Homes. All of the attention made her feel uneasy. She admitted, "The days when we had a lot of people there, I just didn't want to be the main focus. Thankfully, I always have my girls to push attention onto, which they don't mind. I think when the videotaping happened, it felt good to be moving forward, but I didn't want to be talking too much. The military has a thing called Operational Security, or OPSEC. We're taught that you don't display the fact that you're a soldier in communities anymore. They really stressed, 'Don't talk about things. We're here in Iraq and you could become a target.'" Lauren was afraid that all of the attention would expose her to some type of attack.

After the first day, Lauren wasn't allowed back until the project was complete. That way, the TV show could document her surprise and delight when she saw the results. The video footage from that first day shows Lauren smiling as she joined the crew of volunteers and began demolishing sheetrock with a hammer—tentatively at first, and then with abandon when urged on by a volunteer. The foot-age also shows a dumpster being filled quickly with debris: plywood, the old toilet, sink, bathtub, and appliances. In a single day, the crew cleared out eighteen months' worth of clutter and junk, emptying the house so that work could be begin.

Later segments showed the before-and-after transformation brought about by new drywall, refinished hardwood floors, a new bathroom, and finishing touches like new woodwork, and the serene color of blue that Lauren chose for the walls. The video concludes with Lauren and one of her daughters walking into their renovated house for the first time. With a broad smile on her face, Lauren is caught in the footage, "Whoa, this is great! Now, whenever you get inside, it feels quiet and comfortable. It feels complete like a model home." There's a much-needed dining table so that the family can sit down and have meals together. Lauren continued, "It feels good being here. I think that there are going to be good memories made in here."

One of the things Purple Heart Homes did for Lauren's home was provide energy efficient upgrades that will help make heating and cooling the home more financially manageable. We try to provide those energy improvements in every veteran's home. We have seen some improvements that have had as much as $250 a

JOHN GALLINA & DALE BEATTY

month savings because of increased insulation value, updated windows, and more efficient heating systems.

It's clear that Lauren could have never done all of the necessary work by herself, and the power of a supportive community shined through. "I kept trying to make a home somewhere, trying to fit in. This changed my life significantly. My girls and I went from living in a store where every second of the day, I felt as though we were being scrutinized. It feels like we have finally settled down. We could start over as a family and reconnect. My daughter can ride the bus to school now without being bullied. I don't feel like we have to hide where we're living now or who we are. It's life-changing," Lauren shared.

Alex Sawchyn

White Head Farm was the last working farm in Fall River, Massachusetts. Alex Sawchyn, the son of Ukrainian immigrants, grew up on that farm during the Great Depression. He began training as an aviation cadet at the age of sixteen, and eventually joined the Civil Air Patrol in Providence, Rhode Island.

Looking at Alex's face alone, the abundance of history he carries is apparent. In July 1943, World War II was raging. At just seventeen years old, Alex lied about his age in order to enlist in the Aviation Cadets Assistance Program, a subset of the Civil Air Patrol. Alex reflected, "My mother didn't speak to me for years after I did that—she was so angry. Everybody else in my family was so military-minded and possessed the spirit for going after victory. I guess that I was just one of them." The Civil Air Patrol program had been established just one week prior to the Japanese attack on Pearl Harbor, under the jurisdiction of the Army Air Corps. This program would evolve eventually into what we know today as the US Air Force. During World War II, these flyers logged more than half a million flying hours, and saved hundreds of crash victims.

"We flew out of Walter Green Airport to look for submarines. We'd fly all the way to the tip of Cape Cod, turn around, and then fly down to Quonset Point Naval Air Station. As you were flying up, you'd be looking out to the ocean on your right. On the return trip, you'd be looking out to your left. One time, this guy had a couple of sips of some kind of moonshine, or something like that. I didn't see it, but he was flying on his side as he returned. He spotted a big shadow in the water, and sent the Navy from Quonset Point to sink it. That big shadow happened to have been a whale. Later, there was a Smiling Jack cartoon in the paper that read, 'Sighted whale. Sank same,'" Alex recalled with a chuckle.

When asked about what the most valuable lesson he learned while in training, Alex replied, "There's two ways of doing things. You can do it the right way, or you can do it the wrong way. They always wanted to teach us how to do things the right way. There was a lot to learn… you learned so many different things." Alex learned those lessons well, and went on to become an Army Air Corps pilot. He flew numerous, dangerous missions during World War II, including B-29 Superfortress bombers in the Pacific.

After the war ended, Alex remained on active duty, which took him to several continents in support of peacetime efforts, culminating in the Berlin Airlift. After the Nazis surrendered, the US, British, and Soviet military forces had divided and occupied Germany, including its capital, Berlin. Berlin was located far inside of Soviet-controlled eastern Germany, and as the wartime alliance between the West and the Soviets turned hostile, the city became the defining symbol of the Cold War.

Alex Sawchyn with his brother, John, in uniform; a young Alex in Air Force blues

In June 1948, Soviet forces blockaded rail, road, and water access across to the western occupied zones. The US and Britain responded by airlifting food and fuel from their bases in Western Germany to the Allied-controlled areas of Berlin. The Airlift lasted more than a year, carrying over 2.3 million tons of food, fuel, and other necessities. At the height of the campaign, one plane landed every forty-five seconds at Tempelhof Airport.

Twice each day, Alex piloted one of those planes. He remembered the challenge, "It was dangerous because we were using a single runway airfield at Rhein-Main and it wasn't long, only 3,500 feet. You're flying with twelve tons on the aircraft, and you've got to use every available inch for takeoff. Then, you fly to Berlin. During this time, you just had a cup of coffee and then flew back. You were on six hours, and then you were off six hours. You made two trips during the first six hours. That lasted for a year."

While on active duty, Alex contracted acute hepatitis B. He told us, "I don't know how I contracted it. It's either caused by alcoholism, or diseased food or water. I couldn't tell... Doctors said that it might have been from food... Your entire body turns yellow, even your face. You turn as yellow as a bean. Then, your liver gives up and you've got to have constant rest and proteins." He was transferred to Walter Reed Medical Center in Washington, DC. Alex continued, "At that point in time, they didn't know too much about hepatitis, and we were treated like guinea pigs. They were experimenting with all of us. I stayed at Walter Reed for the period of a year. They were feeding me shark's liver, rattlesnake stew, turtle-mock stew, plus I got a lot of shots of all types of stuff." After Alex was discharged from the hospital he retired from military service in 1949.

Alex sits at home with his wife, Theresa, while sharing stories of his exploits during the Berlin Airlift.

Three years later in 1952, Alex met Theresa, and soon they were married. She joined him in Connecticut, and not long afterwards, they bought a house on four mostly-wooded acres at the end of a quiet, dead-end road in Redding. Alex and Theresa raised their two sons there, and it's still their home after more than fifty years.

Over the next fifty years, Alex continued to follow his passion for aviation. When he first returned home after his service, he took a job in Massachusetts teaching students how to fly. Alex founded a Civil Air Patrol unit in Fall River, where he had grown up, and became the commanding officer of the group. In September 1952, he went to work for the Avco-Lycoming Corporation in Stratford, Connecticut. Alex explained, "Avco-Lycoming originally made the engines for B17s. I got a job testing engines on helicopters and tanks. In fact, I tested the first M1 Tank engine. We made between forty-five and fifty-five different types of engines. It got to be a career, and I became Chief of Testing eventually. I stayed there for forty years."

One of Alex's passions, besides aviation, is gardening. He shared with us, "Out of four acres, three were just woodland. Then, I have a beautiful garden. My father came from Ukraine, where the country was called 'the breadbasket of Europe' because everybody would get fed. He taught me how to do the farming. I have a beautiful garden."

In the 1980s, Alex's children bought him a video camera. Since then, he has become passionate about video documentation. He refers to himself as a video historian, and maintains thousands of hours' worth of footage documenting events that honor veterans, including all local parades held on Veterans Day and Memorial Day. He videotapes interviews with individual veterans about their service as well. Alex told us, "In my interviews with servicemen, I always say, 'Don't take it in the grave with you. Spill it out.' I've got more than two hundred personal one-on-one stories of veterans that are going to be given to the historical society."

Alex is proud of his generation's service, and is moved every time he is acknowledged for it. "There's not too many of us still around. We're losing thousands each day throughout the country. I have a cap that says 'WWII Veteran.' I wear that cap no matter where I go; it's my identification. It's mostly older people, but there are a lot of younger people, too, who come over to shake my hand and say, 'Thank you for your service.' They don't even know what the service was, but they thank me anyway. I don't think that I could ever meet other veterans without having tears in my eyes. A lot of them are worse off than I was, and yet they come over and say thank you. I'll tell you, it's a wonderful feeling," Alex shared.

All of the interviews Alex has done with veterans has given him deep insight about their varied service experiences and the challenges they face in their lives. He explained, "Once a month in Cheshire, Connecticut, we have what they call the Air Force Roundtable of Connecticut, and a speaker comes down every time. I've heard about three or four speakers who have come back from Afghanistan or Iraq, and they've given hour-long talks, which I have on cassette tapes. There are a lot of differences. I was in what we now call the Air Force with high-altitude bombing and all that. During World War II, you were either in the Pacific or over in Europe. These guys in Iraq though, they got it really tough. They would talk about how it was 140-something degrees over there and they had to go into their battle maneuvers and stuff like that. It's really rough on the bodies of the guys over there. I mean, not only guys, but women—there's women now. In fact, a young lady who used to deliver the paper to my house, she's a pilot on an F16 up in Washington State, flying planes. There's no limit on women anymore, so they're involved, too."

Alex is active with local veterans' organizations and has volunteered in various capacities for years, often speaking with students at area schools about his service. Alex said, "Before, it was a real patriotic start. Now, it's more educational. I talk to many schools throughout the year. They call me up and ask me to speak." However, what Alex sees taking place in his community worries him. He continued, "We have so many veterans in Danbury, Connecticut. We have a soup kitchen and all of that. We used to go over to the Salvation Army and get older clothes and stuff like that, but they're closing down. It seems as though a lot of people and places are turning their backs on veterans. They want to close down a lot of places because people in there can't keep it up. Five Salvation Army groups are going out of the picture. That was something that all of these veterans were relying on. Now, they don't have those or the soup kitchens anymore."

Last year, Alex and Theresa received a notice from their insurance company, telling them that unless they trimmed several trees, put on a new roof, and painted the house, their homeowners' insurance would be cancelled. Alex told us, "Over the last seven or eight years, we had so much snow and storms around our area. Many trees ended up falling on houses and those houses would lose power. I had an eight-by-twelve shed, and snow collapsed the top of it. The same thing happened to my carport—the roof collapsed due to heavy snow. The insurance companies were losing money because a lot of people put claims in. I didn't put a claim in because I thought that if

I did, my rates would increase. That didn't do any good, because the insurance companies didn't care anyway. Theresa and I had the same insurance company on the house for fifty-four years and suddenly, they cancelled my insurance." Alex knew that he couldn't afford to pay anyone to trim the trees, paint the house, and install a new roof. He decided that his only option was to do the work himself. Climbing ladders is dangerous when you're nearly ninety years old.

Michael McLachlan, a state senator for the area, has been a friend of Alex's for more than twenty years. Michael ran into Alex at an event and noticed that Alex was limping. "I asked him what was wrong, and he told me that he fell off of a ladder," said McLachlan. He advised Alex to stay off ladders. When McLachlan ran into Alex a few months later, he noticed that Alex appeared to be in a severe amount of pain. This time, he had fallen while trying to paint his house for the insurance company. Alex confessed, "I fell off from a ladder and broke my shoulder. It took me a little while to get back into shape, but I still had my right hand. I started painting with my right hand."

McLachlan knew immediately what to do, he went to Alex's house and with Theresa's permission he put a padlock on the ladders. Next, he organized a crew of volunteers and, one week later, they came back to paint the house. Alex was moved, and recalled with gratitude, "Most of the volunteers were veterans. There was about sixteen or seventeen of them. They all had paint brushes, and they painted the entire house in one day."

Alex and Theresa were relieved. Alex went to the insurance company a couple of days later and said, "I painted my house. Can you reinstate my insurance?" They told him that he still needed to put a new roof on his house, den, and garage. Alex remembered, "I definitely didn't have money to do that. That involved about $39,000. I couldn't do that." The couple feared that they might have to sell their house and move into an assisted living facility.

When McLachlan found out about this, he began talking to friends about how Alex and Theresa could get help. Somebody mentioned Purple Heart Homes to him, and McLachlan got in touch with us on Alex's behalf. We had Alex complete the application and the committee approved the project promptly. The next step was to outline the project plan and identify the resources needed to get it done.

A Connecticut remodeling contractor, Steve Thomas, volunteered to serve as the project manager and general contractor overseeing the project. Soon with the help of McLachlan, we were able to round up the volunteers and funds needed, and the project was underway. A wide variety of business owners and other community members were coming together to help Alex showing him just how much he was appreciated and cared for.

One of the many volunteers told us, "When you think about how dog-eat-dog life can be, it's a wonderful thing that this got done. The good deed stuff is really motivating." Another volunteer named Mark owned a roofing company and was also willing to help with the roofing project. He had done several roofing service projects in the past, but not always for veterans. He often replaced roofs for elderly people who have run into tough times and covered the cost himself. Mark told us, "I do a lot of roofs, and if I'm able to help people out, then why wouldn't I do that?" He brought some of the staff from his company to work on Alex's home. Alex recalled, "One morning, I'm sleeping, and I hear a bang—bang—bang up on the roof. There were about fifteen guys on my roof. They tore the whole roof apart and replaced everything. All of the supplies were donated by the local Home Depot. They supplied the lumber and all of the shingles." Jane, another volunteer, even provided chili, hot dogs, bratwurst, and a variety of desserts for the crew; she was from the Weston Kiwanis and neighboring community. Even the dumpsters were donated!

Alex recorded World War II veterans' stories and included filming Purple Heart Homes' volunteers putting a new roof on his home.

Theresa spent that entire day smiling and moving throughout the house, thanking every volunteer she could find. "It's overwhelming. We were in such a bad state and had no idea what we were going to do," she said. Theresa joked that she would be hearing hammers knocking in her dreams because of all the noise on the roof. She said to us, "I'm so grateful for this. If you want to talk about miracles, this is a miracle."

The crew finished the entire roof and cleaned the property all in one day. "It's not about the money," said Mark. "The reward here is that the people are just so happy." Alex was touched by the outpouring of help from his community. He told us, "They just came in and did the entire house. They started at 7:00 a.m. and by 3:00 p.m., they were all done. They cleaned up the whole place. They fixed everything up. There were women from Weston who made every conceivable food that you'd want while you're working."

Finally, the insurance problem was settled. Alex said, "After I got the house all fixed up, I went to another insurance company—the one that I have for my car—and they welcomed me with open arms. I got that insurance right off the bat." He sums up his experience with Purple Heart Homes by saying, "There are good people and there are bad people, but I tell you, every person in that Purple Heart Homes group and everybody else who helped me with the project are one of a kind. You'll never get people like that again in my lifetime."

Helping veterans age in place is a primary goal of Purple Heart Homes. We do this as a way to restore dignity and quality of life for veterans by creating safe, barrier-free environments. A by-product of the work that we do when we bring the community together is a restoration of hope and faith in humanity. Also, it brings dignity to a person's living conditions, where they otherwise cannot provide for themselves.

Alex and Theresa are now able to age in place, in the home that they've shared for most of their lives. Alex shared with elation, "The house looks beautiful. They did a wonderful job. It was all done for nothing. I didn't pay nobody or anything like that. I'm indebted to all of these people. Every place that I go, I mention what happened and what all they did. They took care of this house, and as long as I'm alive, I'll be living in this house." Theresa, who has always been generous in making donations to charitable causes, now makes sure to include Purple Heart Homes in her giving.

Alex still suffers from hepatitis, but he's not letting that slow him down. No longer having to worry about climbing ladders to paint his house or repair his roof, he is turning his attention to the video interviews he has done with other veterans. "I have a thousand cassette tapes. That's my job now. I have a bedroom that was converted into a studio. I've got all of the equipment to transfer from cassettes to DVDs. I'm working on DVDs now," Alex shared with delight.

The Sawchyns' story is a prime example of how Purple Heart

Homes changes lives. Alex said, "I'm going to be able to live here for the rest of my life. I hope that I can live to be a hundred years old, or so. If it didn't happen here, then we would have to be in assisted living. I've visited a lot of friends of mine that are living in them. I wouldn't want to be put in one of them. I'd rather live out the rest of my life in this excellent place where I'm living now. It's all thanks to these guys and what they did for my house."

Lt. Alexander John Sawchyn, 90, passed away peacefully on Wednesday January 4, 2018, in Ridgefield, CT, after a brave battle with cancer.

CHAPTER 7

We're Not Done Yet!

Dale Beatty

When John and I began our mission in 2008, our organization had little awareness and support and completed only three projects by the end of 2010. We've grown significantly since then. By the end of 2017, our organization completed over three hundred projects total, and we just keep growing. Although it's difficult to come up with an exact number, we estimate that more than 70,000 volunteers have pitched in to help, a result of the massive outpouring of effort in communities across the United States, since the beginning of Purple Heart Homes.

We predict that we'll soon be able to complete one hundred projects each year in a sustainable, repeatable operational plan. As each community is able to find success in helping veterans and becomes encouraged to do more, we'll start identifying more and more veterans. They're all around us.

Since the beginning, John and I have had a number of phenomenal mentors in areas such as finance and business, planning and cash flow, program service delivery, production, warehouse maintenance, branding and advertising, and more. We liken the entire experience to getting a college education, and strive to live up to the expectations of our mentors. We cannot express enough gratitude for the people willing to support our dream and vision.

The development of Purple Heart Homes is not solely creditable to the two of us. Our families, friends, individual donors, volunteers, and a host of other people who believe in the Purple Heart Homes mission are the ones who truly sustained our organization. Purple Heart Homes has also received outstanding support from Rotary and Kiwanis clubs across the country. We're also thankful for the financial and volunteer support we've received from other clubs such as the Combat Veterans Motorcycle Association, VFWs, and American Legion posts.

One of our chapter leaders is a thirty-year retired Air Force officer and successful software entrepreneur. He is an example of the kind of person who finds healing and passion by helping us serve veterans in need, and has served as a prominent influence on how we handle our endeavors. We have a number of leaders from other chapters who have joined us along the way and took the time to mentor us as well. We wouldn't be who or where we are today if it weren't for all of the amazing people who have come along throughout our process of helping veterans.

Retired Air Force Officer, Larry Druffel [left], poses with volunteers for the Golden Corner Chapter after a ramp was completed for Army veteran, Wesley Hamilton [center].

From 2010 to 2016, Purple Heart Homes rented a 2,000-square-foot office and a 6,000-square-foot warehouse in Statesville, North Carolina. Things took a leap forward at the beginning of 2017, when we closed on a building of our own. It's a former factory that produced different types of lumber, such as plywood or hardwood floors. The building had been abandoned for several years, and is located in a part of town that is slated for revitalization. Thanks to the hard work of our staff and supporters, we're up and running and able to be a part of bringing jobs and business to our community.

Moving into a building that's nearly ten times the size of our old headquarters means that Purple Heart Homes can spread its wings and continue to grow the number of projects we take on for the veterans we serve. This also gives our organization the opportunity to become more efficient and professional. Increased efficiency has been a consistent goal of ours, and we've focused on stabilizing processes and policies that allow the culture and organization to work more nimbly. Another goal has been to hire other veterans who can do some of the work that has been outsourced until just recently.

Our new space will enable the standardized manufacturing of components such as ramps, modular bathrooms, and other items that are used regularly on our projects. These will be built in Statesville to exacting specifications, and shipped to chapter projects across the country. This consolidation will save time and money, improve quality, and, best of all, exist as a source of employment for local veterans. The years moving forward promise exponential growth in streamlined delivery of components, and will help us serve an even greater number of veterans. A chapter in California could call and say, "We've got an addition that we need to build on this house, but we don't have the funding for it." We could tell them, "We'll send you modular unit number one and you can use that." It's getting the solution into someone's house, yard, or hands much quicker.

Besides its 70,000 square feet, the building also sits on thirteen acres of land. John and I envision the front section of that acreage becoming a veterans' memorial park. Since our organization is unique in that we help veterans of every era, we'd like to have a monument for each war and period of service, so that all veterans are recognized. We have the room, so we definitely want to make that happen.

*Purple Heart Homes staff pose together in front
of the flagpole at their new headquarters.*

Having the ability to own the property indefinitely and develop the projects we prioritize is exciting. Once we've settled in, we plan to use some of the extra square footage for multipurpose spaces that can support other veterans' initiatives, or those of other local nonprofits. John and I also foresee using some of the space for corporations that want to have team-building volunteer events with their employees.

A controlled production environment already arranged means that we can engage volunteers in a space that's monitored safely.

Chapter by Chapter

A Purple Heart Homes chapter is a collection of community leaders arranged as a volunteer organization operating within the culture and guidelines of Purple Heart Homes in order to provide assistance to eligible, service-connected disabled veterans. Chapters concentrate on Veterans Aging in Place (VAIP) projects: renovations or repairs made to homes that are owned by the veteran. Projects vary greatly by the needs of the veteran and the capabilities of the chapter. Typical projects include widening doorways, remodeling bathrooms, building ramps, and installing railings.

By the end of 2017, ten chapters had been established:

- Southwestern New York Chapter (Allegany, Cattaraugus, and Steuben counties)
- New York Downstate Chapter (Dutchess, Putnam, Westchester, Rockland, and Orange counties, plus the five boroughs of New York City)
- Metro Atlanta Chapter (Greater Atlanta area)
- West Michigan Chapter (Mason, Oceana, Muskegon, Ottawa, Newaygo, and Kent counties)
- Piedmont North Carolina Chapter (Guilford, Rockingham, Alamance, Forsyth, Davidson, and Davie counties)
- High Country North Carolina Chapter (Avery, Ashe, Caldwell, and Watauga counties)
- Golden Corner South Carolina Chapter (Seneca area including Anderson and Greenville in South Carolina as well as Athens and Toccoa in Georgia)
- Colorado Front Range Chapter (Fort Collins to Colorado Springs)
- Northeast Ohio Chapter (Lorain, Cuyahoga, and Lake counties)

- Greater Nashville Chapter (Davidson, Williamson, Wilson, Cheatham, Dixon, Sumner, and Rutherford counties)

Starting a New Chapter

Anybody can start a Purple Heart Homes chapter in their own region, and by doing so, will help extend the organization's reach to even more veterans. The process for creating a chapter is relatively simple. Simply go to PurpleHeartHomesUSA.org, then fill out and submit the chapter application form. Purple Heart Homes will then send a packet with instructions on how to develop a board of directors, hold a first meeting, and what papers will need to be completed for the state and IRS. Since Purple Heart Homes has a group exemption for 501(c)3 status through the IRS, new chapter boards do not have to apply separately for nonprofit status. It is extended through the corporate office once the chapter's paperwork is approved.

Adding new chapters will help evolve communities to a new level of understanding the reasons why and how volunteering can make a difference in the lives of veterans and their families on a local level.

Diana Fleming, President of the Colorado Front Range Chapter, poses with Navy veteran, Joseph Brown, who served during the Korean War.

Other Ways to Get Involved

If starting a chapter seems like too much, you can get involved in other ways. You can volunteer for a project if a chapter is already established in your local area. There are many different links on our website at PurpleHeartHomesUSA.org and PHHUSA.org that describe various projects. Or, you can sign up to be placed on our roster for project fundraising, support, hosting third-party fundraisers, and more.

West Michigan Chapter President, Shonda Prow, sitting next to West Michigan Chapter Vice-President, Katrina Serna, at a fundraising event for Purple Heart Homes

Another project subcategory of Purple Heart Homes is Operation Veteran Home Renovation, which falls underneath our Veterans Aging in Place (VAIP) Program. Communities and corporations can engage between August 7 (Purple Heart Day) and November 11 (Veterans Day). Each year between those dates, communities rally together to support a veteran in their area. These events are typically led by corporate sponsors such as credit unions and other community-minded organizations, as well as the Home Builders Association in many areas.

Yet another way to get involved is by simply identifying veterans who own a home who may need a ramp or some home repairs. Anyone can become an advocate for veterans in their community and let us know about them.

It's a paradox. The more Purple Heart Homes does, the more veterans who seem to surface. We know they're out there. The statistics from Veterans Affairs tell us that there are 3.4 million service-connected disabled veterans out there. Many of those veterans are not coming forward, whether it's due to shyness, pride, meekness, shame, or uncertainty. It's not until they see other veterans around them who are receiving help and respect that they're ready to come out and say, "Yes, I need some help, too. Yes, I've fallen on hard times. I'm ashamed of it, but I can't do it alone. I need some help."

There's a powerful pride in adapting and overcoming that's instilled in veterans to be able to press forward. It's difficult for that soldier to come home and suddenly be without a platoon, company, or squad, all wearing the same uniform, singing the same cadence, and marching to the same beat. Perhaps they feel a little empty, or a little lonely, and are uncertain how to overcome their struggles by themselves. It's not Purple Heart Homes that makes a difference. It's the people within the community who rally together that make a difference. Knowing that a neighbor cares—that's what makes a difference.

Often times, a veteran doesn't know how they're going to be treated, how they're going to be responded to. Many of them have thoughts such as, "Are you going to call me a baby killer? Are you going to push a pill on me? Are you going to ignore me?" We think that the basic human desire is the same across the board: Do you see me? Do you hear me? Does what I say even matter? Does what

I've done even matter? Across all generations of our veterans, they simply want to know that they matter, and that they're not forgotten.

John and I realized early on that we, both as individuals and as an organization, can only help so many people. What we want to see Purple Heart Homes do is change the culture within America, so that every community has a Purple Heart Homes chapter and values taking care of every generation of veterans, so as to not allow homelessness within the veteran population to ever happen again. We want to see every American veteran cared for, to see that people are willing to do the hard work that's involved in paying them back for the sacrifices they made to provide freedoms for other nations, and to ensure that our own freedom remains secure.

This effort is going to take more than just Purple Heart Homes. It's going to take entire communities seeing a World War II veteran, a Korean veteran, a Cold War veteran, a Vietnam veteran, an Iraq or Afghanistan veteran—all in the same light.

We recognize that the Purple Heart Homes philosophy is positioned outside the trend of assisting post-9/11 veterans, like many of the charities that have been formed since the wars in Iraq and Afghanistan started, ended, restarted, and continue now with the threat of ISIS. Operating outside that trend has been a true challenge. At many points, we've been questioned by our board, mentors, and advisors (many of whom *are* older veterans) regarding our adamant focus on helping the entire veteran population.

To be honest, sometimes I wonder why we were called to have such a strong focus on ensuring all types of veterans have safe and dignified housing. It's as though the perfect storm formed in our thoughts and hearts and washed us up on the rocky shores of the impact left by generations of combat-wounded, service-connected disabled veterans.

As true battle buddies do, John and I navigated those rocky shores for the first ten years, primarily alone and without a true realization from the rest of society that our particular mission of assisting all veterans carried greater impact to the population of those who served in the ranks of our nation's military. Aside from the servicemen and women themselves, their spouses, children, parents, and other family members are also inherently drafted into serving the cause of defending liberty and freedom, both at home and abroad. It is truly our families who travel with us in our hearts when we put on the uniform. It didn't take long for us to understand the value that a new ramp brought to everyone inside the home—not to mention the influence an outpouring of love and appreciation brings to a community.

After ten years, it would be easy to feel desensitized or complacent with the mission we started. It happens over time. Some people call it mission creep. But over the years, we continue to recognize the multiple layers of impact of a completed project for a deserving veteran family.

It's not just a simple mission for one small (but growing) veterans housing charity—it's also the display and example of social responsibility. As soldiers, we were encouraged to live with the values of loyalty, duty, respect, selfless service, integrity, and courage. While we've struggled personally to uphold those standards, it has been our absolute pleasure to serve those who hold our military values close to heart as well.

Yet again, it's not just the military that embodies values like those listed above. Everyone is capable of the same values that, in truth, can bind us together not only as Americans, but as humans overall.

A soldier in silhouette of the setting desert sun in Iraq

John

Born, raised, and residing in Statesville, North Carolina, John Gallina made his first career move by joining the National Guard, then later becoming a General Contractor. He was deployed to Iraq during Operation Iraqi Freedom II, where he sustained combat-related injuries. Once he returned to civilian life, John refocused his career back to the construction industry before co-founding Purple Heart Homes in 2008, a nationally recognized 501(c)3 public charity. In his free time, John enjoys reading, working on classic cars, and spending time with his wife, Cori-Anne, and their three children. John is also a member of Western Avenue Baptist Church, Rotary International, and serves on a number of local charity boards, such as the Statesville Housing Authority.

Dale

Born on August 7, 1978, Dale Beatty was a native and long-time resident of Statesville, North Carolina. After high school, Dale served in the National Guard for several years before receiving orders to serve in Iraq during Operation Iraqi Freedom II, where he sustained combat-related injuries. When not working at Purple Heart Homes, a charity he co-founded, Dale enjoyed playing drums in his band Outlaw21 and coaching his kids' soccer teams.

He also served on the boards of Fisher House Foundation, USO of North Carolina, and North Carolina Tramatic Brain Injury Council. Giving back to the veteran community was a way of life for him. Dale passed away suddenly on February 12, 2018, due to a double pulmonary embolism. His parents Jerry and Selene, his wife, Belinda, and their three children survive him.